Psychology in Management

McGraw-Hill Series in Psychology
Harry F. Harlow, *Consulting Editor*

Karn and Gilmer   *Readings in Industrial and Business Psychology*

Krech and Crutchfield   *Theory and Problems of Social Psychology*

Lazarus   *Adjustment and Personality*

Lewin   *A Dynamic Theory of Personality*

Lewin   *Principles of Topological Psychology*

Lewis   *Quantitative Methods in Psychology*

Maier and Schneirla   *Principles of Animal Psychology*

Marx and Hillix   *Systems and Theories in Psychology*

Miller   *Language and Communication*

Misiak and Staudt   *Catholics in Psychology: A Historical Survey*

Moore   *Psychology for Business and Industry*

Morgan and Stellar   *Physiological Psychology*

Page   *Abnormal Psychology*

Rethlingshafer   *Motivation as Related to Personality*

Reymert   *Feelings and Emotions*

Seashore   *Psychology of Music*

Shaffer and Lazarus   *Fundamental Concepts in Clinical Psychology*

Siegel   *Nonparametric Statistics: For the Behavioral Sciences*

Stagner   *Psychology of Personality*

Townsend   *Introduction to Experimental Method*

Vinacke   *The Psychology of Thinking*

Wallen   *Clinical Psychology: The Study of Persons*

Waters, Rethlingshafer, and Caldwell   *Principles of Comparative Psychology*

Winer   *Statistical Principles in Experimental Design*

Zubek and Solberg   *Human Development*

John F. Dashiell was Consulting Editor of this series from its inception in 1931 until January 1, 1950. Clifford T. Morgan was Consulting Editor of this series from January 1, 1950 until January 1, 1959.

PSYCHOLOGY IN
MANAGEMENT

Mason Haire

University of California

SECOND EDITION

McGraw-Hill Book Company

New York   San Francisco   Toronto   London

Psychology in Management

Library of Congress Catalog Card Number 63-20446

To V. R. H.

PREFACE

In the organization and operation of a business there are necessarily a number of assumptions about psychological principles. A business is—at least partly—an integrated collection of people. So-called "management principles" are, therefore, bound to be built on beliefs about the nature of people, what motivates them, and how best to direct and change their behavior, their attitudes, and the like. Unfortunately, we seldom examine these implicit assumptions in great detail. We have lived with them so long that they go unnoticed and unchallenged. It is useful, from time to time, to look at these bases on which our thinking rests.

The aim of this book is to give an overview of psychological problems in management. In this way the book helps to bring out some of the principles of behavior that underlie modern industrial practice and give us a chance to examine them in full light. The main objective is to give a pattern and coherence to the psychological underpinnings of managerial practice in dealing with behavior. It is not a "how to do it" book; there are few specific solutions to specific problems in the field or in the book. Rather it is a "how to think about it" book—one designed to stimulate new insights and new perspectives.

The book is called *Psychology in Management;* the field of which it is a part is often called "industrial psychology." There is an important difference in the terminology. The traditional title of the field—industrial psychology—implies that the problems are industrial and specific applications are drawn from psychology to attempt to solve them. When we speak of psychology in management, on the other hand, the rephrasing implies something different. We are concerned with psychological problems that appear in an industrial

setting; that is, instead of specifics selected from psychology
to solve particulars in an adjectivally limited field, the whole
range and power of theoretical concepts in psychology are
available to deal with behavior in industry. The shift in
thinking from industrial psychology to psychology in industry is one of the major changes in the field in recent
years. This book, therefore, is organized first in terms of psychological principles, and then, in later chapters, in terms of
their appearance in the context of various industrial problems.

The first edition of this book came out in 1956. A great
deal of development has taken place since then, and I have
tried to bring the new thinking to bear on all the topics
treated. In 1956 there was barely a recognizable field of
industrial social psychology. Now it is booming. Organization theory was little discussed; now it is a central issue. A
few scattered experiments marked the course of thinking.
This number has grown tremendously and reshaped many
ideas about psychology in management. All of these changes
and influences are reflected here. I, myself, have encountered a group of new problems—in industry, in the laboratory, and in theory-building. These, too, have had their
effect.

An attempt has been made to aim this book both at the
practicing manager (at all levels of supervision) and at the
college student interested in industrial psychology or business administration. For this reason it examines both the
psychological problems and the industrial situation in some
little detail, although it presupposes a certain amount of
knowledge of each. The reader is urged to approach the book
actively, not passively. Do not sit back and wait for gems of
truth to be thrust on you. Go at it vigorously. Ask it questions. Do these things occur in situations with which you are
familiar? Do the general principles fit the problems you have
been dealing with? Probably the most important part of the

time spent reading a book is the few minutes just after you stop reading. Stop when you've closed the book and before you go on to something else. Ask yourself what you've read, what it means, where it applies, why the author said what he did and the way he did, and how it fits with your thinking. If you will do this with this book—or any book—you'll multiply the effectiveness of your time manyfold.

It is impossible for an author to state his indebtedness fully. My main obligations for the content of this book are to Douglas McGregor, of the Massachusetts Institute of Technology, and Edwin Ghiselli, of the University of California, though they can in no way be held resonsible for its shortcomings. I have always realized how much my thinking owes to these two men. As time goes by, I realize it more and more fully and more deeply. Debts of this sort are only gradually understood and never discharged. My more general indebtedness for all the things that make work possible and interesting is expressed in the dedication.

MASON HAIRE

CONTENTS

Psychology in Management

CHAPTER 1

INTRODUCTION

This is a book about people at work. It considers both business problems and behavior problems. Since it is basically a psychology book, it tends to approach the processes of business through the behavior of people. Human factors are not, of course, the only problems of business, but they are a large and central part, and they are becoming more pressing. Here we ask how to deal with some of them. The first part of the book deals with some general characteristics of human behavior. Then it goes on to take up specific business problems in the light of these broad principles. First, however, we need to see the general issue in perspective. We need to ask why we deal with people in a book about business. That is the focus of this chapter.

There has been an increasing interest, beginning just before World War II, in the general area that has come to be known as "human relations in industry." More and more, industrial management all over the country has moved into this field, with leadership conferences, Job-Relations Training, employee-relations training, and the like. To a certain extent this interest is part of a cycle of fads in personnel techniques, and in terms of the fad, the present interest is probably near the peak. There are, however, several other developments in our industrial organization and industrial economy which suggest that the growth of interest in the problems of relations between people on the job is rooted in long-term and important forces and will be with us for a good while. In many cases, the rising pressure of these forces suggests clearly that it is high time we directed more attention to the nature of human beings in our work force, and to the problems of the relations between people on the job.

Is this a book about human relations?

Many people looking at it will tend to ask, "Is this *nothing but* another book on human relations?" The "nothing but" seems to mean that it is a tired old argument that one can see through and around and that can be dismissed as such without consideration. It is worthwhile, because of this, to look at the development of the human-relations movement a little. In broad terms, it began after the war. In its early days its proponents seemed to suggest that people ought to be given more satisfactions at work because it was a Good Thing. It seemed to be a kind of moral pressure—people *ought* to do this. Economists and practitioners of business administration tended to reply, "Making people happy isn't the business's business. Let them be happy on their own time." This led to the question of whether human relations would make money, and to the relationship between morale and productivity. Countless studies finally made it clear that the relationship between morale and productivity is not at all a simple one. It seemed more than ever as if the human-relations-ers were just urging that people ought to be happier at work on humanitarian grounds—it was better that way.

Actually, the human-relations movement probably sensed, in the early days, a series of changes going on inside and outside the business which forced more attention on the individual at work. At first the issues weren't perfectly clear, but they gradually settled down. Within the business, the industrial engineering tradition worked in the direction of rationalizing jobs. The early steps brought mostly increased efficiency, but their continuation began to change the job and the individual's relation to it. Improving the job began to take away the man's desire to do the job and his feeling of himself in it. At the same time, outside the business, standards of living and standards of education were rising. In general social and political terms the role of the individual was being increased. As he got more understanding and skill, and as a tight labor market and a strong union gave him more security and more bargaining power, it became clear that more place needed to be found at work for the individual's drives, loyalties, and characteristics. The early human-relations argument was probably responding to a sense of these broad sweeping changes, although it wasn't easy to state them in these terms until time gave us more perspective. The problem can be stated in somewhat different terms today. Increased attention must be given to the problems of people at work—not just because it is a Good Thing, but because the development of both business itself and the society in which it operates demands it. Behavior theory is an essential part of management theory.

Technological progress and human-relations progress

One of the clear and present pressures in business today arises from the technological character of Amercan industry. We have today in America an industrial machine of vast productive potential, but one which is primarily built on technological change. Our national genius has been for introducing new methods, machines, and processes to speed and improve production and to make it less expensive. Historically, our big strides have been made by virtue of changes that are oriented to the characteristics of the machine, the process, or the material. We have improved production tools, methods, handling techniques, and the like, and thereby greatly increased productivity. To do it our industrial plants have been geared to the machine. We operate a machine on the basis of the kind of power input it requires and its potential output, its optimum speed, its demands for lubrication and rest, and the best environment for its operation. In general, our engineering sciences have vast and detailed knowledge of the characteristics of the machine just down to the end of the handle—the point at which the operator takes hold of it.

To a large extent, our knowledge and interest stop at the point where the operator enters. If we operated the machines in our plants knowing as little about their power requirements, output potential, lubrication, and the environment in which they work best as we do about the operator, we should very soon have widespread and drastic breakdowns. When we curse the whimsicality and undependability of the human operator, we should be thankful for his corollary flexibility, which is the thing that allows us to operate with such a high margin of error in our personal decisions. There is a crying need for a scientific study of the characteristics of people in industry to parallel our understanding of mechanical characteristics, so that we may maximize the efficiency of both partners of our industrial potential.

Our industrial production layouts are built to utilize the production technique, the machine's characteristics, and the material's qualities to the utmost. The operator is considered the dependent variable. He is expected to (and fortunately does) bend and adjust. It is interesting to speculate on what might happen if we were to build a production line designed to maximize the human resources and motivations of the operators, and then consider the machines as dependent variables which must be built to conform to the requirements of a system designed to maximize the human's potentialities. It is possible that such a development might tap tremendous reserves of productivity, but it would take a very great deal more understanding of the characteristics of people at work than we now have. Common industrial practice has not put great emphasis on an increased understanding of the variables involved in the way people work. If we were to get a new machine in a plant and were uncertain about it, we shouldn't think of putting it on the line and running it without finding out a lot about it. It would go to the engineering or research department for exhaustive study so that we should know how to run it. For some reason, with a new human, about whom we may in fact be equally uncertain, we don't worry about characteristics, abilities, skills, and potentialities. We assign him more or less at random, and if he does not work, we get another.

Technological change has meant, primarily and essentially, the linking of the productive efforts of large numbers of people and the consequent multiplication of their effectiveness. In doing this, we have built industrial organizations consisting of very large groups of people and created entirely new problems—new in both kind and size—in the techniques of social control. As our organizations get bigger, more complex, and more interdependent, they threaten to generate problems that far outstrip our means of coping— our understanding of people and the ways of dealing with them.

Because of our tradition of thinking of the technological character of business, we often fail to see that the big recent steps have not been in production or processes. They have been in management technology. The changes in techniques of management and distribution have done more to revolutionize American industry quietly in the last fifteen years than engineering changes. The so-called "team concept" of management and the suburban supermarket have had the kind of effect on our industry and economy today that work simplification and production lines once had. Developments are being built today on the basis of organization and management techniques. To move into the future we need to build further on these bases.

The small manager, before World War I, had face-to-face techniques for human relations in the industrial organization. Some of them were good, some of them were bad, but by and large the intimacy of his organization meant that a knowledge of the results of his actions was fed back to him reasonably soon, and he could modify his practices with some hope of learning. Today we approach a situation where personnel practices have such far-reaching ramifications that by the time their effects—good or bad—are felt, they are too far away to identify them precisely. It is probably also true that the large organization not only has made the problems more difficult but has actually created problems of a new kind which are possible only in large-scale organizations. We must move toward their solution, or the technological developments that have made our industry great may have in them the seed of its destruction. Politically and economically we may be slipping now toward ends that are inherent in too great a gap between the problems generated by the kind of human relationships implicit in large mass-production industries and the kind of techniques we have for dealing with people.

The survival of an enterprise depends on its successful continuous interaction with a variety of outside "publics"—customers, suppliers, stockholders, employees, the community, and the government. The continued freedom to manage depends on the success management has in adapting to this multifaceted outside world. This isn't often made explicit in managerial philosophies, but it is more and more widely recognized. Twenty-five years ago a speech beginning, "The objective of business is the production of goods and services at a profit . . ." would have meant grave agreeable nods from a group of executives. Today it would seem hopelessly out of date. It would be necessary to begin by saying, "The company has responsibilities to its stockholders and its customers, its employees, and its community. . . ." This has been part of a broad change in the feeling of social responsibility which management is willing to accept. In a funny way, it isn't socially acceptable for most managers to speak about their policies being based on a feeling of social responsibility. By tradition, managers are supposed to be "hard headed" and to think only in terms of what makes money. When they do things for other reasons—community growth, employee safety, and the like—they usually say, "*In the long run* it will make profit by creating a better environment for the company." It may be fortunate that we don't balance our books in the long run. The motives for many of these actions seem to be a broad realization of management's social responsibility, whatever reason is given. In general, management behaves much better than it speaks.

As our industrial plants have grown bigger we have had to build organizations with more ramifications and complexity. An organization, however, is a set of relationships between people, and it exists for the purpose of accomplishing the ends of the institution. As we have created new and bigger organizations we have created new problems. Today's industrial managers face a job that is different in kind as well as in degree from that of a generation ago. As we get into more complex hierarchical structures, it becomes more and more true that each man deals only with his subordinates and not with the actual product. This inevitably means that a greater weight must be attached to the skills and abilities that he has in dealing with people.

It has been said that mankind's ability to destroy is growing according to an exponential function, while his techniques of social control are increasing only linearly. The sharp edge of the conflict between these two developments has been felt quite keenly by many of our atomic physicists, who are appalled at the implications of their technological inventiveness and at the lack of a workable mechanism to regulate the utilization of their developments. If we had made as much progress in social control from the League of Nations to the United Nations as we have from the use of TNT to Nagasaki, the problem would not be so pressing. It is just because our understanding of human relationships has failed to keep pace with our mechanical developments that it presents a compelling problem. Roosevelt, realizing the implications of this disparity, said in the last speech before his death that the world must develop a science of human relations if it is to survive.

In industry we may parallel the exponential curve of destructiveness but with a less easily recognized destructiveness than the spectacular atom and hydrogen bombs. The results of expansion in size and increase in complexity continue to present problems, and the magnitude and importance of the problems increase exponentially, while we may be optimistic to think that our techniques of dealing with them are increasing even linearly. To the extent that we have been successful in our technological changes, we sharpen the need for an increased understanding of the nature of people at work and the processes of human interactions in groups.

Human-relations implications of an interdependent culture

Another development which has emphasized the need for increased understanding of human relations has been the radical change in the American economy and the American culture in the last fifty years. We have gone from a country with many small craftsmen and a host of self-employed to a country whose industrial organization is characterized not necessarily by mammoth plants but by medium-sized groups that go far beyond the small owner-managed businesses of a generation ago. This development may be the natural outgrowth of industrial technological change, which often requires a larger organization to utilize effectively and economically the developments of new machines and processes. It seems to be an irreversible process. Our industrial units will probably continue to get larger.

Among other things, this development means that our whole culture, both industrial and nonindustrial, is moving in the direction of a more and more highly interdependent society. We are no longer as self-sufficient as our fathers were. In the home, technological developments in processing and distribution techniques have relieved the housewife of many arduous jobs of baking, preserving, washing, and the like. But, at the same time, they have made her more dependent on the regular schedules of the baker, the laundryman, and the supplier of frozen foods at the market. As we progress, we can no longer do for ourselves. We build a more complex and hence more interdependent society, where each plays a specialized role and depends on the other to carry out his role. We are becoming a society that lives by taking in one another's laundry. To see how widespread and close-knit our interdependence is, we have only to look at the dislocation caused by a power interruption, a flood that cuts off transportation, or a strike in the processing and distribution systems. An interesting example of this is seen in the results of the United States Strategic Bombing Survey in Germany. It was found that the most disastrous effects of bombing on the Germans' morale occurred when the sewage and utility systems were destroyed. Their dependence on the paraphernalia of modern society made them most vulnerable. If we had a weapon that would disrupt the enemy's means of dealing with one another, we would have a tool of unheard-of effectiveness. As we become more complex, we depend more and more on one another, and our relations with others become more and more important for the smooth working of the system.

Industrial organizations are moving in the same direction. Our technological advances mean more and more that we are developing a race of specialists—none of them self-sufficient and all of them highly interdependent on one another's skills and processes. As is the case in nonindustrial society, this interdependence means that all the way up and down the line of our industrial organizations, managers must have ever-increasing skills and insight in handling interpersonal relations.

The role of increased job security in human relations

The internal organization of our industrial plants has changed, too, and these changes put increased pressure on our human-relations techniques. When a given man is hired, now, it is much less likely than formerly that he will be let go for having failed to work out well on the job. Formal labor-management relations and contractual obligations make it harder and harder to eliminate individuals from the work force for any reason other than a general reduction in personnel. This is not to suggest that these changes are not beneficial in a general social sense. In many cases they have forced the revision of personnel policies that were arbitrary and whimsical. However, they have added problems to our relationships.

At the simplest level, it means that people are going to be around longer on any given job, and with a continuing relationship, the nature of the relation and its fruitfulness become more important. Two other very important things come from this development of more certain tenure, however, which will have to be developed in more detail later. In the first place, it means that management must count more on utilizing the skills and abilities that are present in or can be developed in the present work force. It is less and less possible to rely on replacement to improve the quality of the work group. This means an additional emphasis on training and leadership in the development of people on the job, and this in turn puts more weight on the problems of the relationships among people. Still more pressure is put on the problem of the relationships by the fact that as a worker begins to feel secure in his job and sure of his continued pay, other things—his feeling about his superiors, about his fellow workers, and about himself and his job— become more important to him. All these things combine to force us to pay more attention to our human-relations techniques, and to ask ourselves searchingly whether we are developing the requisite skills fast enough to keep pace with the developing problems.

Why we have tended not to examine our human relations in the past

One of the chief reasons why people shy away from a straightforward examination of their human-relations techniques is that, to a much greater extent than is true of other fields of technical specialization, every man is his own psychologist. Life is such that we all of us have come to some conclusions about what kind of motives make people work and about how to deal with them. The result is that we are much less apt to modify our existing notions for those of the trained worker in the field than we are in the case of, for instance, electronics or chemistry.

We are particularly wedded to our own psychological concepts because they have been built up over a long period of

time, and our techniques of dealing with people are peculiarly our own. Indeed, our ways of dealing with people are
the expression of the intangible that we call "personality."
We may notice that when we describe someone—"He is
friendly, trustworthy, amusing, thoughtful . . ." or "He is
hostile, aggressive, withdrawn . . ."—we are using words that
describe the way he behaves in his relations with others. Our
personalities are a summary of our techniques in human
relations, and as such they are very close to us and not freely
exposed to earnest scrutiny. Moreover our ways of reacting
to people and of working with them have often been built
up in traumatic and unpleasant circumstances, so that the
force that keeps us from looking at them squarely is strength-
ened. We have all learned methods for dealing with snubs,
with deference, with domination, with stubbornness, and the
like, and the techniques have been internalized and made
part of our own ego-defenses so that we tend not to examine
them.

In the industrial hierarchy the situation is even more compelling. In the general case, the superior, at any level, is in
the position he is because of the degree of success he has
had in dealing with others. He is what he is because of the
techniques of human relations. Since his success and security
depend on them, it engenders too much anxiety for him to
question whether or not the techniques he used in dealing
with others are the best possible. To challenge them is to
challenge the foundations on which his present success is
built. It is perhaps for this reason that "success" courses and
"personality" courses are most supported by those who feel
that they are not particularly successful in their relations with
others. Actually, to the extent that a man is a success in a
hierarchical organization, he underwrites more responsibility
in dealing with people, and it is the more successful, rather
than the less successful, who could most profitably utilize an
inventory of current skills and the improvement of a train-

ing course. In addition, these changes are different from many other innovations in management. When we accept new procedures or processes it usually means that someone else does the changing. Human-relations changes mean that management changes. There is often an understandable reluctance because of this.

One other large barrier customarily opposes the explicit examination of techniques of dealing with people—an ethical question. It is often objected that an analysis of ways of working with people and an attempt to acquire skills in dealing with them are manipulative and hence morally wrong. "People shouldn't be pushed around by high-powered propaganda techniques that make them do things they don't want to, or by subtle psychological skills that mislead them concerning why they are doing things." A good deal of this objection seems to disappear when we separate the skills themselves from the ends to which they are employed. The utilization of skills to manipulate people toward ends that are not in their best interest is reprehensible, as is the use of certain kinds of motivational levers that are culturally taboo. This, however, should not logically condemn the investigation of, and improvement in, techniques of dealing with people in general; indeed, in a human society, they are not optional. We are born into an interdependent environment, where we cannot provide for our own needs, and we are successful to the extent that someone else provides for them. As the individual grows and takes a place in a more complex society, he is even more dependent on others, and his survival is completely dependent on the degree to which he can get others to do certain things for him and to accept certain services from him in return. We are inextricably enmeshed in interdependence. Consequently we must achieve many of our needs *through* others and they through us. There can be little room to question whether it is right to "use" others in this way. We must work through others to survive.

The moral issue relates to the way in which we "use" them and the ends to which we "use" them, but not to the basic fact of manipulation. Since we must work through people, it behooves us to acquire sufficient skill at it so that the relationships can continue and can function smoothly and fruitfully.

The role of human factors among management's problems

All these considerations force us more and more to an increased consideration of the problems of relationships among people in industry. This is not to suggest, however, that problems of human relations constitute the main problem in industry or that improved social techniques will offer a cure for all of management's problems. We seem to have tended, in industrial personnel thinking, to drift from panacea to panacea in a search for solutions. We have had fanatical devotees of efficiency systems, rationalized wage-payment plans, multiple management, and the like, many of which seem to have been presented as a remedy for all ills. It is not suggested here that an understanding of human relations is such a universal medicine, but an attempt will be made to describe, in its proper perspective, one of the forces acting on a business.

We need to see an industrial organization as an organism imbedded in a field of forces. It has many pressures within, and the forces that are pushing and pulling inside it may well be characteristic of the particular business: the history and tradition of the plant, the nature of its product or the raw material, the investment per worker required to tool for production, and the like. There are a host of problems of this sort within any business which are definitive with respect to a single organization and which provide pressures characteristic of the particular plant. The plant is also subject to another group of stresses and strains from outside; it is imbedded in a field of forces which play on it from outside and which also shape its problems and help to determine the appropriate solutions. Its competitive position, its position in a local labor market, its relation to the community or to the resources on which it draws for raw materials may be important pressures. The combination of all these forces, internal and external, provides problems which are special to each plant and organization, and makes it virtually impossible to offer general solutions which apply to all. A change in one of the factors influences the operation of the others; any change must work toward maintaining a kind of equilibrium in these forces which is necessary for continued working. In these terms, the problems and remedies must be surveyed for particular plants at particular times. General solutions are dangerous and difficult.

In very broad terms, there is a kind of cyclical shift in the problems that are central to the enterprise. The relative importance of different issues waxes and wanes as the nature of the business changes. Years ago the major problem was capital formation. The organization and personnel and controls of the firm tended to reflect this. Money became easier and the focal problem shifted to production. New people and new processes became dominant. Engineers, control of production, and measures of productivity became paramount. Financial influences carried over, of course, but their role diminished. Presidents began to come from the line management rather than the bank or owner. They had slide rules in their shirt pockets (figuratively) instead of piping on their vests. The production problem, however, is rapidly becoming routinized. It is no longer the vital issue. But high volume production has supported large companies, and the focal problem is shifting to organization. The trick now lies in the organization and direction of large groups of people complexly related to one another.

We need to see business questions—and answers—in

terms of the issues that are paramount. Many people still think of a company primarily as a place that makes something. The "dark satanic mills" of nineteenth-century England remain as an image. They express a time when the Industrial Revolution's main concern was production processes and the main social consequence was the grinding physical hardship of work. The time has disappeared and the problems have changed. They are probably better expressed today with the American concern with the Organization Man. The process is moving inexorably on. After capital, production, and organization, the next cyclical peak seems likely to be distribution. With the production problem solved, the issue will be to get rid of the product. A firm that thinks of itself mainly as a place to make things, or one which concentrates too much on a neat organization in the distant future, will probably be as out of date as the Dickensian accountant on a high stool wearing sleeve garters and a green eyeshade.

In the midst of all this, however, we can count on having with us in any organization a group of people who must maintain a high level of efficient interactions for the business to run smoothly. The problem of the effective utilization of the human resources of the plant is one that is most common to all, though the particular solutions may not be the same from case to case. It is to this area of the set of problems of a business that this discusion is directed. It may have greater or less weight depending on the particular plant and the particular time, but it will always be a point that must be checked and evaluated as a trouble spot in an audit of the external and internal forces shaping the success or failure of a business. The business will have, as one element, a reliance on the productive efficiency of a group of people. If we can understand the nature of these people better and know how to use this understanding in management practices and policies, we can work toward the control of one of the factors in the complex set of problems presented by a modern business organization.

The role of theory in management

All managerial policies have a theory behind them. Most managerial policies—about personnel, pay, consumer motivation, leadership, and the like—flow from a theory of behavior. On the other hand, most managers like to say, "Let's talk about something practical. I don't want any theory about it." This usually means that there is a theory implicit, but the person doesn't want to examine the assumptions behind policies and practices. To get a general base for action we need a theoretical framework. Innovation—in management as in other technologies—stems from theory. Theory provides the standards by which achievements are judged. We need theory in management, and this book will deal largely with behavioral theory related to business problems.

In behavioral theory there is one special problem. To the suggestion that it is relevant to business, the manager often counters, "Ah, but you can't change human nature." This is, of course, substantially true. However, human behavior and behavior patterns do change markedly as the context of behavior and the conditions of people change. Further, our advance in managerial theory depends not on changing human nature, but on understanding it, utilizing it, and, to some extent, controlling it. One cannot change the law of gravity, either, but with sufficient understanding of it, it can be utilized to do some remarkable things. Our aim is not to make human nature obey a particular method of managerial control but rather to seek the managerial method that will be appropriate to human nature, that will utilize it in the processes of business.

□□□□□□□□□□□□□ □□□□□□□ □□□□□
□
□
□
□   # THE NATURE
□
□   # OF PEOPLE
□
□
□
□
□
□

In order to know more about the nature of people at
work and to see more clearly the factors that underlie their
interactions in the work situation, we must look at some of
the basic principles having to do with the nature of people.
There is no attempt, in this chapter, to present an exhaustive coverage of the principles of human behavior, but we
must touch briefly on some of the areas that are particularly
relevant to the problem of human relations in industry. We
shall have to examine with particular care three fields that
come into all our experiences with human beings in the
work situation: first, the problem of learning and the way
in which behavior is modified; second, the kind of motives
that activate behavior; and finally, the way in which people
shape their attitudes about the world around them.

The problem of learning and the Law of Effect

We are constantly faced, in industry, with the problem of making changes in behavior. The job of management is very seldom to keep people doing exactly as they are doing. Usually we either want a group of people to start doing something that they aren't doing now, or to stop doing something that they are doing. Almost always, the big problems come in changing behavior. Since a large part of human activity is involved in the process of modifying behavior patterns and shaping them so that they will be more nearly goal-oriented, it is important for us to look at the processes that occur and the principles that govern them, so that we may utilize these principles efficiently in producing changes.

Psychologists speak frequently of a principle of learning which is called "the Law of Effect." It means, simply, that behavior which seems to lead to reward tends to be repeated, while behavior which seems not to lead to reward or seems to lead to punishment tends not to be repeated. It is not a particularly complicated principle, but it is very important in shaping behavior. For some reason, we all seem to be able to keep it clearly in mind and to use it in practice when we are, for example, housebreaking a dog, but when we become involved in more complicated situations in human interactions we lose track of it. The principle is exactly the same in human behavior, and it is essential for us to see it clearly in the cases in which we want to modify behavior.

It is part of the superior's role in a hierarchical organization that he controls many, if not most, of the rewards that are available to subordinates. All people at work are looking for the satisfaction of many of their needs. We shall have to go into the kinds of needs that motivate people a little later on, but the fact remains that everyone is constantly striving for need-satisfactions. It is part of the nature of the situation that, at work, the superior controls many of the means to need-satisfaction. By the proper use of his control of the means for need-satisfaction, he can provide or withhold rewards at appropriate times. When we remember the principle of the Law of Effect—that behavior which seems to be rewarded tends to be repeated, while that which seems not to lead to reward or seems to lead to punishment tends to be eliminated—it is clear that the superior has a great opportunity for shaping behavior. Indeed, whether he is conscious of it or not, the superior is bound to be constantly shaping the behavior of his subordinates by the way in which he utilizes the rewards that are at his disposal, and he will inevitably modify the behavior patterns of his work group thereby. For this reason, it is important to see as clearly as possible what is going on, so that the changes can be planned and chosen in advance, rather than simply accepted after the fact.

An example may make the point clear in its application to industrial practice. It is not at all uncommon to hear members of management describe a situation in which two applicants for a promotion are nearly equal in merit. The poorer one, however, let us say, has considerably more seniority. Although there is leeway in the contract for a promotion on the basis of merit, the man with the greater seniority is promoted, in order to avoid argument. It is also not at all uncommon to hear the same people say at another time, "Our biggest problem is that people don't try hard any more, the way they used to. They used to figure that if they worked hard they'd get ahead, but now they just figure that if they wait long enough they'll be promoted, so they sweat it out rather than trying to do a good job." The members of management, in these cases, are not entitled to express surprise or dissatisfaction at their subordinates' performance. The reason the subordinates produce the kind of behavior they do is because they have been trained to behave that way. They have been shown that rewards come for seniority and not for merit. According to the principle, the behavior that seems to lead to reward tends to be repeated, while the behavior that seems not to lead to reward tends to be dropped out. The way in which the reward is administered determines the behavior.

This does not mean that rewards for seniority are bad. Long service deserves compensations. However, in order to produce the kind of behavior we want, we should not let it become confused with other kinds of reward that are properly designed to encourage other types of activity. Protection by virtue of seniority is a reward for certain kinds of behavior which we want to encourage, as well as an obligation to the senior worker. However, if we want to encourage quality in performance, in addition to simple long-term service, we should be careful that the rewards for the two do not overlap, and that they do not compete with each other. Clear-cut rewards must be retained for merit and must be clearly structured so that they are seen as such.

A similar situation develops in all kinds of small everyday administrations which do not seem, at first glance, to be rewards or punishments, but which operate that way just the same. We often hear it said, "The men in the work force don't ever give a thought to ways to do their jobs better." We think of this as a general characteristic of a group of people. But have we trained them to act this way, or have we, on the other hand, provided actual rewards in practice for just such thinking about the job? When someone approaches a foreman with a suggestion about something to do, does the foreman imply by his tone and manner, "Your job is to do the work— I'll do the planning"? This can be as effective a punishment, or at least lack of reward, as many more carefully planned acts, and these small everyday occurrences are the day-by-day administrations of reward and punishment by which the superior shapes the behavior of his subordinates. Underlying the process throughout, we have the principle of the Law of Effect: that behavior which seems not to lead to reward, or to lead to punishment, tends not to be repeated. As we go on to other problems and practices of dealing with people we shall see this principle coming into play repeatedly.

One often hears members of bank managements complain that their tellers are not sufficiently zealous in building good customer contact. They wish the teller would realize that the bank's continued success depends on the customer, and make him feel welcome and well treated. Too often, they say, when a depositor approaches the window, the teller gives the impression that he has been interrupted in an important job (if, indeed, the customer hasn't been made to wait while the teller finishes adding his column of figures) and that the customer will throw his figures out of balance by making a transaction. Why does this kind of thing happen? The members of management might well ask themselves whether they have trained the tellers to do just this and, if so, whether this is the way they should be trained. The teller has found all his rewards in the past for careful balancing of the books, and his punishments for failures in this line. He has probably never been rewarded or punished for his treatment of customers. Under these circumstances, an understanding of the Law of Effect will let us predict certainly what will happen. Those behaviors which seem to lead to reward (balancing the books) will tend to be repeated; those behaviors which seem not to lead to reward (dealing with the customers well) will tend to be eliminated. The bank will suffer. Because of the overriding nature of the problem of control within banks, they have often slipped inadvertently into a policy which they would never make explicit: balancing the books is the only important thing. From this implicit policy has flowed a daily training which has taught the teller how to behave: balance the books at all costs; anything which interrupts that task is a liability. There has never been a real decision to train the tellers this way, but the silent focusing on the problem of control has put it into the actions of every level of management, and because the subordinates are subject to the operation of the Law of Effect, it works as a training policy.

What could be done differently? No one would ask that management adopt a policy that it doesn't matter whether the books balance, as long as the customers are happy. As in the case of the example a little earlier concerning promotion on merit or seniority, both aspects of the teller's work are important. Rewards must be provided both for his balancing and for his customer contact, and they must be kept separate and distinct, so that it is possible to create a situation where both kinds of behavior tend to be repeated. In order to do this it is necessary to be clear and explicit about the aims of the business, about the things that need to be done, and about the rewards that are provided for doing these things. Otherwise we slip into the situation of inadvertently training out an essential pattern of behavior.

One further point should be made clear before we leave the Law of Effect. We must be careful to notice that it is stated that "behavior which *seems* to lead to reward tends to be repeated, and behavior which *seems* not to lead to reward or *seems* to lead to punishment tends not to be repeated." It is not always true that the behavior which in fact leads to reward, or which was the boss's reason for providing the reward, will be seen to be the path to reward by the subordinate. If the reward occurs too long after the behavior, it may be ineffective; if the connection between the behavior and the reward is difficult to see, it may be ineffective. Moreover, in many cases the subordinate may mistakenly assume that a reward came for a particular bit of behavior which was not at all what management intended to reward. We shall see in more detail later on how this problem of the subordinate's making sense of the world and organizing things in his own mind complicates the picture. Here we need simply to realize that the effective rewards are those that he has put with a particular bit of behavior. In addition to providing reward and punishment, management must accept the responsibility for seeing that the appropriate connection between behavior and reward is appreciated by the recipient of the reward.

There is some evidence, in the laboratory, that those behaviors which are followed by reward tend to be repeated whether or not the individual is aware of the connection. Learning is probably not as effective in this situation as it is when the connection is clear, but it is not impossible, either. This means that in many cases where it is difficult to maintain a close contact in the employee's mind between behavior and reward—where the situation is too complex, or the time too long, or the like—it is still possible to rely on the operation of the Law of Effect. This kind of "silent" operation of the principle only points up the responsibility of management for the consistent provision of rewards in modifying behavior.

It would be well, at this point, to say another word about the operation of reward and punishment under the Law of Effect. We have so far spoken of them as if they operated equally, but in the opposite directions. This is not quite true. While it is true that those behaviors which seem to lead to punishment tend not to be repeated, it is also clear, in laboratory experiments, that the most important effect of punishment is to produce variability of behavior, so that it becomes possible for the superior to provide reward for the desired behavior and hence increase its likelihood of repetition. Often the response to the positive side of the Law of Effect seems to be, "It's very well to talk about rewarding the kind of behavior that you want repeated. What do you

do when it occurs so seldom that you don't get any chance
to reward it?" It is just here that the role of punishment is
most effective. The consistent application of punishment in
the face of undesirable behavior leads the person to try
other kinds of behavior from his repertoire of responses,
and this variability makes it possible to find and reward
the desired behavior.

The nature of needs

When we turn to the field of motivation we find another
set of facts that are useful in considering the problem of
people at work. All the behavior that we see around us is
directed by a striving for the satisfaction of needs. All of life
is a struggle to satisfy the many needs that everyone has,
and it is a never-ending struggle, because the human being
is built in such a way that as soon as he partially satisfies
one or two needs several others are pressing on him and de-
manding attention. All the individual's life is spent in trying
to satisfy his various needs, and the direction of his behavior is determined by the multiple pressures of the several
needs that are acting on him at any one time. Since these
are the determiners of behavior, we must look more closely
at what they are and the way they work, in order to understand and deal with the behavior they produce.

There have been many descriptions of the kinds of needs
that motivate human behavior, and many lists of needs have
been worked out, ranging in length from explanations of all
behavior in terms of two or three basic needs to very long
lists that seem to account for each specific act by a new
need. It is tempting to try to explain all behavior with a
single motive. The sweeping simplicity of the process is attractive, and many of the widely popular theories are of
this type. Freud relates everything to a libidinal drive, Jung
to a drive to assert and clarify one's ego, and Marx to an

economic determinism. Tempting as these single-motive theories are, when we assert that everything is basically something else, the process of transformation becomes so complex that the theory loses reality and usefulness. It is probably impossible to say at this time what is the correct list of needs, or how many there actually are. We simply do not know enough about the things that motivate human beings to give a final answer to the question, "What kind of needs and how many of them are there?" However, we can group them in a way that makes it possible for us to handle them, in a manner that will give us some insight into the way they work, and in particular, into their operation in the industrial setting.

The classification of needs that has been developed out of his clinical experience by Dr. Walter Langer in *Psychology and Human Living* provides just such a useful tool. Dr. Langer distinguishes among three classes of needs: physical needs, social needs, and egoistic needs.

Physical needs are the ones we are most familiar with, because they are the most easily observed. They include the "tissue" needs—the needs that are built into the organism as a result of the way the body is constructed. In this class we would put the needs for food and water, for air, temperature control, sleep, elimination, and the like. They are the most obvious needs that we observe in humans, and they are the things that we take care of first with the dollars-and-cents pay that we take home from work. We buy food and shelter of various kinds as a minimum prerequisite of existence, and in order to satisfy the most primitive of our needs.

The second general class of needs is that of the *social needs*. They are the needs which find their end product in a particular relationship with other people. We might list, for example, such a need as the drive for affiliation, for association with other people. It has been variously referred to as "the herd instinct," "gregariousness," and the like, but at base it points to the fact that man finds a satisfaction in associations with others and feels a real deprivation when it is not possible. We do not have to look far to see this need at work in determining behavior. People are continually showing evidences of it in their family relationships, in their club activities, and in their patronizing crowded beaches on their vacations. All of us have felt the desire for companionship and, conversely, the pangs of loneliness. Indeed, the fact that solitary confinement is an extreme punishment for the recalcitrant prisoner is a testimony to the strength of the motive.

The evidence of the operation of the need for affiliation at work is not hard to find. We see it in many studies of morale and in casual observations showing the importance that is placed on "a good bunch" at work, and most of us have chosen at one time or another to sacrifice certain aspects of a particular job in order to take advantage of the presence of a preferred group of people at some other job. For example, studies in the automobile industry have shown that the number of grievances a man files is associated with the number of people in the work group. The man who works alone has the most grievances—lacking opportunities for social need-satisfaction. Men in groups of two or three have the next most grievances, and larger groups have fewer. In laying out production lines to meet the requirements of the process, we have often done violence to the group. We create a situation similar to the "strip" towns that have grown up in a long thin line along the highway in comparison with the "circular" towns that used to grow up around the railroad station. In the stretched-out line, interaction is harder, group formation is inhibited, and the fabric of social satisfaction is partially destroyed. The force of the need for affiliation in the industrial situation becomes even more clear when we see the compelling effectiveness with which a group can put pressure on one of its members who, let us say, exceeds the tacit group-set level of production. When he goes to the locker room or the washbasin and finds that conversation stops and people turn away from him, or when he walks home alone repeatedly, the deprivation provides a potent force to bring him into line.

Another need which has as its primary aim a relationship with others is the need for affection—to be both the recipient and the giver of affection. Throughout all relationships, from early interactions with one's parental family to a man's own family in adult life, the need to be the object of affection and to be affectionate toward someone else plays a large part. It is often evident in less clearly marked forms in many friendships and loyalties that are marked by stronger bonds and a more individualized relationship than is characteristic of a simple need for affiliation. It may even be that this need supplies the motive power for a feeling of loyalty toward institutions and companies, and that part of the return that an employee finds in feeling wanted and cherished by his company partakes of the need for affection.

Our need for nurturance also falls under this heading. Again, it is a need that works in two directions—we have a need both to care for someone else and to be cared for ourselves—but it is a social need in that it is primarily oriented toward a kind of relationship with others. The things that flow from it are commonplace—the pleasure one takes in looking out for the welfare, comfort, and safety of others, and, conversely, the pleasure that we all take from time to time in relaxing in the attention that someone else gives to our needs.

All these are social needs, and there are many more of them. It is hard to say how many more of them there are or just what they are. They include all those motives determining behavior that have their origin or their end in establishing a particular relationship with others. They have a wide field of application in human behavior, both at work and outside of work, and it will pay us to examine the operation of these needs in the industrial situation later on.

The third group of needs falls under the head of *egoistic needs*. They are distinguished from the social needs by the fact that their goal is not primarily a relation with other people, but primarily a particular view of one's self or ego. Other people are often the means for egoistic need-satisfaction, but the end is primarily in a condition of one's self. For instance, a need for dominance may be thought of as one of the egoistic needs. To be sure, other people are necessary in the achievement of dominance, and in this sense the relation with others is important, but it is the fact of domination that supplies the motive power of the egoistic need to the dominator.

Egoistic motives are the things that are satisfied when one can give a satisfactory answer to the question, "Who am I?" They tend to be answered in the first person. The statements, "I am ..." "I have ..." "I am recognized as ..." are all indicators of these drives. Egoistic motives are satisfied by recognition, by status signs, by being able to tell others what to do, by being set apart from the group, by being admitted into the inner circle, and the like. William Whyte, in his insightful *Human Relations in the Restaurant Industry*, tells of a case where the kitchen of a large restaurant was threatened with a work stoppage because the woman in charge of preparation of sea foods was going to walk off the job. A detailed look at her problem showed that her main complaint was that in the organization of the kitchen she was called the "fish woman"! She refused to do this work. She was perfectly happy to do the same work as "in charge of the preparation of sea foods," but not as "fish woman." Who we are and how we can see ourselves and how we see others see us provide very important satisfactions and deprivations to us. We joke about calling the grease pit a "lubritorium," but it may well have psychological meaning.

To be able to drive a company car provides satisfaction well beyond that involved in the sheer convenience or dollars-and-cents saving on transportation.

Another example of the operation of egoistic needs in an industrial setting may help to make the meaning clear. A plant with a largely routine operation stood very low in productivity in the list of a group of such plants operating in various parts of the country. Management took a number of steps to correct this, none of them connected with the technological aspect of the business, and soon brought the plant to the top of the list. Two of the things they did are particularly relevant here. In the first place, there had developed a tendency, as there often does in such operations, for the foreman to call the personnel office in the morning and say, "Number 11305 isn't here today; I need a replacement." When the personnel office said, "Who is that?" the foreman might say, "How do I know who it is? It's Number 11305—send me another guy." The lack of individuality in the foreman's view of Number 11305 could probably be felt by the man and so deprived him of a certain measure of egoistic need-satisfaction. It is not only when, in a movie, the headwaiter calls a customer by name that he seems to be a bigger man; on the job the minimum of recognition is at least to be recognized beyond "Hey, you." In this case, each foreman was given a personnel card to fill out on each of his men. He was asked to list the man's name, address, wife's name, how many children, what age, previous job history, hobbies, etc. The most important direction was that the foreman had to fill out the card without the man's knowing that the foreman was getting the information! When he had the card filled out, the personnel office could throw it away; they already had the information. The real good was done when the foreman came to see his men as individuals instead of as "Number 11305."

Similarly, as many men as possible were given training on

jobs other than their own, even though the company found it cheaper to replace turnover by hiring in from the street than by transferring from another part of the line. It didn't help the company's personnel problem directly, but it did give the man a feeling of growing and accomplishment. Advances such as these in the provision of egoistic need-satisfactions probably materially aided the company's improved production.

As was the case with social needs, there are many egoistic needs. One might mention the need for achievement that is present in some degree in everyone, the need for acquisition, the need for autonomy, and the like. Again, it is hard to say exactly how many egoistic needs there are, and what they are. They encompass all those needs motivating human behavior whose origin springs chiefly from an attempt to improve one's view of himself. Each of us can be thought of as operating in terms of an "ego-ideal"—a set of values and ideals in terms of which he sees himself. All the behavior that builds him up in the direction of this ideal provides need-satisfaction in the service of egoistic needs.

The "economic" motive

A word should probably be said at this point about the so-called "economic" motive. It comes up so often in these problems that we should deal with it here. In the terms in which we are speaking, *there is no such thing as an economic motive.* There are a great many motives and quite a few different kinds of motives. In general, none of them demands a specific substance for satisfaction. Hunger demands food. Bread, milk, meat, etc., will all satisfy the need, though not necessarily the appetite. (The so-called "special hungers"— need for salt, eating dirt, and the like—are relatively rare and separate cases of tissue needs.) When we are hungry, we may get our food through a cafeteria, but there is no cafeteria motive. Similarly, we may get our food through the use of money, but the drive is for food, not money. Money is important. It is even more important, in understanding behavior, to understand the variety of purposes served by money, and to be clear about the motivation.

Frustration and conflict among needs

All human motives can be classified under these three headings, and we can use this systematization to examine more closely what kind of motives are operating in the work situation. We tend to pay, primarily, in terms of physical need-satisfactions. We pay in terms of dollars and cents with which one can buy the means of satisfying hunger, thirst, and the like. There is no question but what there is often a good deal of egoistic need-satisfaction in dollars-and-cents pay, particularly if the pay is large, or large relative to that of one's friends, but the primary return of pay is physical. There is a host of opportunities for social and egoistic need-satisfactions at work, and they necessarily serve a worker as part of his pay. Consequently, it is important for us to look at jobs to see whether they are constructed so that the rewards of social and egoistic need-satisfactions are geared to producing the kind of behavior that is desirable in terms of the institution's objectives.

In many cases we have constructed situations that pit these need-satisfactions against one another, rather than harnessing them together, so that the result is a conflict that detracts from the motive force of each need and places the worker in a frustrating situation. An example of this kind of situation was referred to before, in the case where an incentive-pay system promises a worker more physical need-satisfaction in return for more work, but does it only at the expense of his social need-satisfaction if he violates the group culture by exceeding the group norm of production.

When such a situation is allowed to occur, the amount of dollars-and-cents pay that has to be paid out to produce unit increase is disproportionate to the return, if it can be effective at all in producing an increase. It is equivalent to driving with the brakes on. It is inefficient in the extreme, and in many cases the situation can be restructured so that the social need-satisfaction is accomplished in return for the same behavior as the increased physical need-satisfaction. Wherever the group can be brought to see higher production levels as a group goal, for instance, the two motives will work together instead of against one another.

A good example of this conflict between physical need-satisfactions on the one hand and social and egoistic need-satisfactions on the other is to be found in *Man on the Assembly Line,* by Charles Walker and Robert H. Guest. In a detailed study of workers at an automobile assembly plant, it was found that the median earnings of workers was about $60, compared with a median of $42 on their last job. On the other hand, a survey about what they liked about their present job and their previous job showed that six times as many people mentioned disliking their assembly-line job as mentioned disliking their previous job; three times as many people spoke of liking their previous job as spoke of liking the assembly-line job. They are getting more pay for doing what they don't want to do. The two kinds of need-satisfactions are opposed, and the result is to pay more in terms of physical need-satisfactions in order to compensate for the deprivations of egoistic and social need-satisfactions that are involved in the assembly-line job. Walker quotes them as saying things like, "I'd take any job that would pay the same amount of money . . . ," "I'd prefer a job off assembly-line work . . . if I could get the same money." These comments sound like men who are settling for more money in return for less of something else. What else are they losing? Of all the things these men spoke of as liking on the assembly-line job, 95 per cent were pay and only 5 per cent were the job content; on their previous (non-assembly) job, about 50 per cent of the "likes" were pay and 50 per cent were job content. When the psychological characteristics of the job are investigated, the picture becomes even clearer. Repetitive jobs were mentioned as "disliked" 9 to 1; the more different operations on a job, the more it tended to be liked; many men complained that the lack of a chance to talk and joke with other men was one reason for not liking the job. These aspects of the job description are all things that flow from the deskilling which minimizes the cost of turnover, the routinization and mechanization that increase the productive efficiency of the mechanical aspects of the plant. Are they equally efficient in human terms? As one clue to this we might notice that the automobile industry, where these developments are at their most extreme, pays an average wage 25 per cent higher than the average of all manufacturing. This sounds very much as if it is necessary to pay more to make up for other things the job lacks. We might well ask whether it is not possible to build a job layout that will maximize human motivation as well as mechanical effectiveness.

Similarly, we often pit social and egoistic need-satisfactions against one another. Many times men avoid or refuse an opportunity for advancement to foremanship, suggesting that they don't want the extra responsibility, or aren't good leaders, or the like. In many cases it seems probable that the opportunity for self-aggrandizement inherent in a promotion to foremanship is actually threatening to cut the man off from social relations with his group, and in the face of the conflict he chooses the latter rather than take the promotion and lose his affiliations. The effectiveness of increased pay (physical need-satisfaction) and increased ego-aggrandizement in the job lose out in competing with the social need.

When we begin to see the opportunities for social and

egoistic need-satisfactions at work, they seem to spring up all over. There are many opportunities for social relations at work that do not necessarily interfere with production, and it is often possible to increase greatly the feeling of group membership on the part of the work force and thereby provide real social need-satisfaction. In many cases, we should severely question those production layouts, working rules, and practices which have grown up and which act to limit social relationships on the job. They seem, often, to have had their origin in an unformulated notion that if people enjoy something it can't be good for them and must be interfering with production. This is exactly parallel with the notion—a remnant of our Puritan culture—that medicine, to be good for you, must taste bad. No one could formulate and defend that notion explicitly, but how many of us betray a hidden faith in it? Similarly, many management practices seem to be based on the theory that, for instance, inspection lines should not be set up so operators face one another because they will chat all day, and when they are standing around having a good time they are *ipso facto* not doing their work. Perhaps if we were to maximize the opportunities for social interaction at work we would greatly increase the over-all return the employee gets from the job and thereby improve morale and consequently his view of the job itself.

An example will illustrate the kind of thing that is involved here. In a large central office of a utility, it had been the practice to operate a single large room full of girl clerks —100 of them—sorting bills as they came in from the service line. The work was relatively tedious and exacting, and the department had always been one where turnover, absenteeism, and mistakes were real problems. The company eventually changed the layout of the workroom as a part of other work on the building. The single large room was now broken up into a series of rooms, with about ten girls in each room. Although the nature of the work was the same, the absenteeism, turnover, and mistakes all went down. Instead of being one of a very large group, without any individuality, each girl was now a member of a small enough group so that she could see herself as a person in it. Instead of feeling, when she woke up in the morning with a cold, "I'd better stay home, they'll never miss me," she may now have felt, "I'd better go in anyway; Mary and Sue and Jane will have to do my share if I'm not there." The old organization minimized the opportunities for either social or egoistic need-satisfaction. It is hard to feel that you are an important member of a group of 100, and friendships almost inevitably lead to cliques. On the other hand, the new layout of the work facilitated both a feeling of association with the individual members of the work group and a feeling of individual importance, as the individual changed from being 1 per cent of the group to being 10 per cent.

The same kind of principle works in the reverse direction. In the British coal industry it was the practice for many years to have the workers mine in small teams. A "hewer" and his mate, with perhaps the assistance of a boy, would make a separate contract with the management to work a particular area of the face of the vein. These men did the whole job—drilling, blasting, picking, loading, and transporting the coal. They worked as a close unit and depended on one another. Subsequent technological developments made it more economical to mine by the "longwall" method, according to which the work was divided into shifts. A longer section of the seam was worked at a time, and a group of forty to fifty men worked at once. One shift drilled and blasted; a second dislodged the coal; a third filled the cars and transported the coal to the surface. This change meant two things psychologically. In the first place, it destroyed the primary face-to-face group whose members depended on one another for both safety and production. In the second place, it spread the men out geographically so that the structure of the larger group was even less accessible to the men. The result of these changes has been a considerably increased accident rate; bad feeling between the shifts, who tend to blame the last shift for the condition of the workings and for safety hazards; a kind of overindividualism, which destroys much of the cooperative spirit on the job; and the like. While the change has some technical improvement, it has been introduced at the expense of some real liabilities in the psychological climate on the job. Social need-satisfactions have been severely limited, with attendant difficulties. One wonders whether it would not have been possible, with more mature consideration, to introduce a plan which retained the technological advantages of the new system, without working so inefficiently with respect to the motive power of the individuals.

It is instructive to ask why it is that the boss sometimes seems to work longer and, in some ways, harder than the subordinates. Or, similarly, we might ask why it is that many workers will do a mediocre job on a production line all day and go home in the evening to sweat blood building a perfect boat in a bottle. A large part of the answer may be in the fact that the job means something to the boss that it doesn't to the subordinate, because it has social and egoistic need-satisfactions for him that are not present in the way the subordinate's job is set up. The boat in the bottle plays a very different role in the need-satisfactions of the hobbyist from the work product that he makes all day at the shop. We have more and more shaped our production processes so that we must pay for output chiefly in terms of physical need-satisfactions to the exclusion of all others. It seems doubtful if it is psychologically possible, even if it were not prohibitively expensive, to provide enough dollars-and-cents pay to substitute for the social and egoistic need-satisfactions that are possible and that should be made available in work.

We need to ask ourselves searchingly whether jobs can't

be improved in these respects. Are there the opportunities for social interactions that are possible without interfering with production? Have we developed all the opportunities possible for egoistic need-satisfactions in the form of problem-solving possibilities, opportunities to acquire skills and knowledge, chances to advance relative to one's ego-ideal? In many cases these opportunities are not present because the subordinate's need-satisfactions in these areas seem to conflict with the superior's. Many a superior has increased his own egoistic need-satisfaction by achieving a momentary dominance as he says, "Come on, break up the gabbing and get back to work," but it is worthwhile questioning whether the resulting increase in production offsets the loss entailed by the effect on the employees of the deprivation involved in their submission to domination and the inhibition of their social satisfactions. Another common phenomenon occurs when superiors at all levels of the management hierarchy hoard information and tell their subordinates "only what they need to know." To do this greatly increases the ego-aggrandizement of the superior. It is a hallmark of the superior that he knows more of the over-all picture than the man lower down. Consequently, to hold back information shores up and makes more secure the superior's superiority. It may hamper the subordinate's work either directly in his lack of information, or indirectly in his lack of feeling that he has an over-all view of what he is doing and that he is in the confidence of management. But it does pay rewards to the superior when he can say, with a knowing look, "Well, we've got some big plans that you don't need to worry about. You just turn out the widgets and we'll take care of the rest of it." We only need to question whether it is worth it to the company to have him feel that way.

It is certainly clear that these kinds of motivational problems are not peculiar to subordinates. Managers have egoistic motives, too, and their satisfactions are an important part of the company's over-all activity. We only need to wonder whether they are being obtained in the most effective way. There is certainly an egoistic satisfaction in the mere fact of being boss, of being the number-one man, of being the one to whom the others must come for direction. Indeed, if it were not for this kind of return, it probably would not be worth it for the boss to be the boss. The responsibility and work are so great that we could not afford to pay enough dollars and cents to make it worth it. The manager needs the egoistic satisfaction. In some cases, however, it may interfere with the satisfactions of others. There are still industries in America where a junior executive must ask permission to marry. In banks this may be rationalized on the theory that if a man marries when he is making too little he will be tempted to put his hand in the till. However, the restriction on the man's autonomy in a very personal matter is extreme, and it may deteriorate into a case where management goes far beyond the needs of the situation in determining what action the subordinate can take. This may well provide gratification to the superior but at considerable cost to the employee. On the other hand, many large organizations have explicit formal policies about the size of desk and the length of nap on the rug that goes with an executive position of a particular level. These outward signs of status are rewarding to the man who advances in the hierarchy, and may provide him with a fair part of his pay for working without being as expensive to the person who doesn't have them. Status symbols are effective only to the extent that they imply that people below that level don't have the status, but they do not affect those lower down as directly as in the case of management's decision about marriage, for instance. Throughout, we must realize that the same motivational principles apply to superior and subordinate, and both must achieve satisfaction in the same organization.

These are the kinds of places where we have failed to take

account of the full range of human motivations in designing work situations, and these and others like them are the areas that we must scrutinize carefully for improvement in opportunities for social and egoistic need-satisfactions, for it seems clearly impossible to attempt to substitute physical need-satisfactions for all the others that are possible. What does it cost to design a production layout where no one knows his role in the over-all finished product, but only tightens a clamp? It may well be a more efficient way to handle materials, but is it a more efficient way to handle people? What does it cost to design an operation so that it is clear to the men who work it that the requirements are being built so that anyone can do the jobs, and each man is almost immediately replaceable from the labor pool? It must detract from his creative effort to feel that his individual contribution and skills are not essential, and it must add greatly to his insecurity to feel that no amount of effort and improvement can make much difference in his indispensability. Changes of this sort seem not only to involve costs in dollars and cents, as we increase wages to make up for other satisfactions, but to cost irreplaceably in terms of a different attitude toward the job and toward one's self that is growing in production industries.

One of the major effects of our technological progress has been the deskilling that is its almost necessary concomitant. In an odd way, technological change usually takes away personal skills, may demand a higher degree of company-trained skill, and often involves a greater responsibility for the process. When a man could do something with his hands, it was *his* skill. Often it is replaced by something like a complicated interpretation of dials and gauges. It may, in a sense, be a higher level of skill, but it is no longer, in quite the same sense, *his* skill. It is the machine's skill and the company's skill. The consequences of his actions may be more far-reaching than before—responsibility may be increased. This often only serves to exacerbate the feeling that he no longer controls it. As we take the skill of the individual out of the job we lessen his egoistic reward. We also rob him of a dependence on himself in many ways, since his peculiar abilities are no longer so necessary, and the job has been built to replace him with maximum ease. In view of this threat to long-term security, and the fact that he cannot depend on himself, it is no wonder that there is a growing tendency to demand fringe benefits from the company. The demand for contractual security is a natural outgrowth of the fact that the man has been deprived of the kind of security that comes from his own peculiar worth. When he can't depend on himself in the way he once could, he must have contractual assurance that he will be taken care of in the future, that if he is sick he will be paid during the period when he can so easily be replaced, and that his unemployment will be underwritten by someone. In the face of these deprivations, a demand for security arises which strikes the company, the state, and the national government. It is one of the pressing social problems of our time to know what aspect of the social organization should accept the responsibility for replacing the kinds of security which deskilling and technological progress have stolen. Our increased standard of living is built on this kind of change. We must face the social price it costs, however, at the same time that we are accepting its benefits.

In addition to the demand for security that arises from this depersonalization that comes with deskilling, it seems likely that much of the motivation for union organization comes from the same source. In the face of technical developments which rob the man of his individual bargaining power by depriving him of his individual worth, the only solution is to band himself with others to regain the power he may have had before. Big business grows from technological change and from the need to amortize the cost of change over a large volume. Its psychological implications breed big unionism equally surely. Again, we cannot enjoy the fruits of improved methods without devising new social techniques to contain in our society the by-products of the change. If we keep these relationships in mind in considering the nature of people at work, it may help us to understand the development of today's industrial pattern.

The hierarchical character of needs

One aspect of the dynamics of the way in which motives operate needs special emphasis in connection with the problem of motivation at work. As we look at the three classes of needs, the physical needs clearly seem to be more basic, more fundamental, more elementary than the social and egoistic needs. This relationship often leads us to believe, erroneously, that if sufficient satisfaction is provided at the basic level there is less need for satisfaction of "higher-order needs," or that the satisfaction of social and egoistic needs can have a substitute value for the satisfaction of basic physical needs. When these viewpoints are expressed in terms of the industrial environment they mean that if jobs are plentiful, wages good, and tenure secure, relatively less attention need be paid to the other need-satisfactions, which then seem to have somewhat the aspect of froth or window dressing. Again, it is sometimes thought that when wages are low, jobs insecure, and working conditions physically poor, enough attention to social and egoistic need-satisfactions can compensate for the inadequacies in physical need-satisfaction. Both these propositions seem to be based on a mistaken notion of the hierarchical character of needs.

It has been said that man does not live by bread alone. The emphasis that is placed here on the provision of social and egoistic satisfactions is in entire agreement with the first implications of the statement. However, it has also been pointed out that man *does* live by bread alone—when there is no bread. Because of their fundamental character, a threat of deprivation to the basic physical needs makes them all-pervasive and compelling as motives and temporarily eliminates the action of higher-order needs. The explorer, lost in the desert, is primarily motivated by thirst. He places little premium on companionship as such, and the status of his ego-ideal is of relatively little interest to him in comparison with his desire for simple survival. The threat to his existence by deprivation of physical need-satisfactions temporarily crowds out the importance of higher-order needs. When he finds his way again, and feels secure in the attainment of food and water and shelter, his needs for affiliation, for achievement, for nurturance, and the like may again take on paramount roles.

The same situation occurs in our industrial culture. As our jobs become more secure because of labor-management agreements, as pension plans and social security provide for our futures, the potential threat to future satisfaction of our physical needs is very much lessened. The opportunity for other need-satisfactions, and consequently their force, increase. It is for this reason that the current social gains in working conditions, Federal old-age plans, a full-employment economy, and the like greatly increase the pressure that is put on management to provide opportunities for satisfactions in the higher-order needs. In the face of serious threats—local unemployment, gross inflation, and the like—we can expect a reduction in the role of social and egoistic needs as the basic physical needs resume their primacy. However, barring such developments we can probably expect the physical drives to seem to recede, while other motives assume a greater relative importance.

It does not follow, however, that the primary drives have, in fact, assumed a less important role. Many morale studies in industry have grossly underestimated the importance of physical factors because current conditions of security with respect to physical need-satisfactions remove these motives from the center of thought and give more place to other drives. It is a quite common finding in recent morale studies to see that, among the things that are important at work, wages rank eighth or ninth in a list headed by such things as "a chance to work without too much supervision," "a good bunch to work with," and the like. We would be very much mistaken if we took this to mean that wages are, in fact, not particularly important to the employee. In a period of relative security they are taken for granted. They are an essential, but they are assumed, so they are not mentioned. It is also assumed that the foreman will not use a whip, but it is taken for granted and not listed as one of the reasons for liking a job. However, if wages or the security of employment were threatened, the physical needs would quickly crowd to the head of the list, in a position commensurate with their primary role in the human's make-up. When physical needs are well satisfied, and when their future satisfaction seems secure, the situation puts more emphasis on the provision of opportunities for satisfaction of the higher-order needs. If basic needs are threatened, they will resume their original primacy and it will not be possible to provide substitute satisfaction in the form of social and egoistic needs. To overlook either of these propositions and their operation in the industrial situation is to mistake the nature of the interrelationship among needs, and to slip into serious mistakes in dealing with people at work. At the present state of our social gains with respect to job security, the first of these two propositions is operating: under a condition of relative certainty of physical need-satisfaction, an increased emphasis must be placed by management on the provision of opportunities for higher-order satisfactions.

It might be pointed out that a somewhat parallel situation exists with respect to the objectives of the firm. Whenever we discuss managerial practices, someone is sure to say, "Ah, but do they make any money? After all, profits are the

reason for being in business." Although the parallel is an
analogy, without any apparent internal necessity, this seems
exactly like saying of a man's behavior, "Ah, but does it get
him any food? After all, getting food is the reason for living."
Food is necessary to sustain life and profits are necessary
to sustain corporate existence. When either of them is
threatened, they become the single all-important factor—
until the threat is eased. When food—or profits—becomes
relatively secure at a level adequate to ensure life, other
objectives become important. For the company, this means
that they look beyond to their multiple responsibilities and
objectives. It is as misleading to consider profit the single
objective of business as it is to consider hunger to be the
single human drive. In a sense we may say, in parallel, a
company does not live by profits alone—except when there
are no profits.

The development of needs—dependence and independence

One more point is worth looking into, in considering the
motivation of men at work: the development of needs and
the central role of the balance between dependence and
independence in human behavior. The human infant is born
into the world with a full set of physical needs, but without
the equipment to satisfy them for himself. He is completely
dependent on another agent to provide all the means for
need-satisfaction—indeed, all the means for survival—for
him. All of us know, in some measure, in adult life, this kind
of dependence, and it has some very comfortable aspects,
for it means that one need not worry about one's own wants,
since their provision is someone else's province. When we
go to the hospital we feel a little of this situation. There is
nothing to do but lie there while the nurse brings food
and magazines and cigarettes, and one of the most comfortable aspects is that there is no pressure to do anything for
yourself because you can't take care of yourself. Eventually,

this dependence becomes frustrating and irritating, because the same dependence on someone else to provide for you which means comfort also means that you are dependent on, and at the mercy of, the other, and there is nothing you can do about the failure of the agent to provide for your needs. You want to "do for" yourself.

In whatever language, this problem must face the developing infant very early. As he is accustomed to signal that he wants something by a lusty yell, and to receive instant satisfaction, he relaxes into the comfort of dependence. There must come a time, however, when perhaps baby yells and mother starts to him. Just then the telephone rings and she goes to answer it. Now the infant can begin to experience not only the frustration that is involved in being dependent, but a very basic threat, since (at whatever level he realizes it) his very existence depends on the intercession of an agent to provide for him. As a result of this juxtaposition—the fact that the infant is born with a set of needs, but is dependent on an agent to satisfy them—there grow up simultaneously two contradictory groups of drives—one in the direction of dependence and one in the direction of independence.

Many of the social needs seem to develop with the dependent side of the balance. Faced with the fact of a dependency, it seems natural that a desire to attach one's self to other people would arise in infants, and that the need for affiliation might arise simply because of the increased security involved in the presence of other people who can serve as agents to minister to needs. At very early ages it may be that the presence of someone else, and particularly relationships with others, has a value in that it guarantees that someone else will be present to provide the means for need-satisfaction. It would not be surprising if there grew out of this drive for a relationship with others to assure satisfaction, a drive in the direction of strengthening the bond of the relationship and making the attachment between one's self and the other person as strong as possible, to assure the continued relationship. This may provide the nucleus for the later development of the drive for affection. Similarly, at this time, the need to be nurtured—the need to be taken care of—is present in the dependent relationship.

At the same time, there is a growing awareness of self in the infant and a growing desire to escape from the threat that is implicit in dependency by being able to take care of one's self. In these origins of independence we begin to have a large part of the future personality of the individual, a development that is intimately connected with his egoistic needs. He begins to develop a need to have autonomy and to care for himself as a measure of protection against the insecurity of dependency, and with this come a greater meaning of self and a drive for control over his environment and other people, and the roots of many of the things that will later appear as egoistic needs.

This concept of the development of needs is elaborated here for several reasons. For one thing, it helps us to understand the nature of the needs and their role in the individual's adjustment to life later on. For a second thing, it helps us to see that the problem of the balance between dependence and independence is a task that each individual faces in his development, and to realize that each of us is still marked by the particular degrees of dependence and independence that he achieved in formative periods. Consequently, each of us places different weights on the various needs that spring from these two sources, and has different problems in coping with any of the things that are related to dependence—submission to authority, surrendering of autonomy, self-determination, and the like. Finally, it is important to see the origins of dependence and independence in infancy because they parallel so closely the situation in which the subordinate finds himself at work that we can profit by their examination.

The superior controls most of the paths to need-satisfaction. The subordinate must, in the nature of the case, depend on him for many of the things he hopes to accomplish at work. Consequently, he finds himself in a situation that is very like the infant's dilemma, and the similarity is more than mere analogy. An understanding of the one can greatly aid us in understanding the problems and processes of the other. In industry, as in the home, the dependence is not only a problem for the subordinate. Just as the mother must shape the child so that he leaves his complete infantile dependency, in which he cannot accomplish anything for himself, and still curb the development of his independence so that it is possible for him to take suggestions and live with others, so the superior in an industrial hierarchy has as one of his important problems that of achieving a healthy balance between the dependency that is inevitable in the situation on the one hand, and an active independence that will raise the subordinate above the level of the zombie without making him intractable on the other. Dependence is essentially passivity. In many cases companies seem to think largely in terms of the "loyalty" of employees. Loyalty in many senses may point to just this kind of passive dependence: a relaxation in the attachment to the institution. Other kinds of managerial leadership—the wise use of suggestions, of participation, and the like—can develop a kind of independence which provides initiative rather than passivity. We shall find this to be a central problem when we consider the problems of leadership and supervision in industry in a later chapter.

The organization of the environment and the development of attitudes

There is one final area that we must examine before we leave the general field of the nature of people: the way in which people organize their environment—the way in which they decide what attitude they will adopt toward people and things. There are three outstanding basic facts that we must remember if we are going to be able to understand human behavior. The first is that the environment itself does not provide an organization. If we make a separation between the physical world outside of us, on the one hand, and the psychological environment, or the world that we see, on the other, we come to see that the order and organization is not in the physical stimulus but in the observer, and that one of man's greatest problems is to make sense of his environment. The second fact is that man's behavior depends, not on what is actually out there, but on what he sees; not on the way the world is actually organized, but on the way he organizes it. This is at first a deceptively simple point, but it is probable that more misunderstandings in human relations arise from this than from any other single factor. The third point is related to the other two: man has a great deal of anxiety attached to his organizations of the world. Man's environment is not organized in itself; he must organize it. His organization determines his behavior. His behavior, and its appropriateness to the environment, determine whether he will be successful or unsuccessful—in many cases, whether he will survive or not. For this reason, he is reluctant to give up any organizations that seem to work, because of the danger that is involved in being lost in a disorganized environment.

The first point seems the most paradoxical: that there is no order in the world around us except that which is supplied by the perceiving individual. We are so accustomed to being able to distinguish things from not-things and to having stability in our world that it is hard to think of any other possibility at the simplest level. Indeed, at the most simple level, human beings seem to be built in such a way that a given set of physical stimuli elicit a fairly uniform response from one person to another and within one person from time to time. We have the capacity to distinguish figure from ground; smooth-flying contours seem to be part of the same "thing"; similar objects seem to belong together; and the like. We have relatively good agreement on the way things look.

When we look at the world we often have to add to it to make it make sense, and to provide the order—the "thing-ness"—which is necessary for us to be able to deal with it. There is a group of dots below. It is almost impossible to say that there are six dots, three on the left and three on the right. We tend to see them as pairs, and the pair-character of the dots is as real in our experience as the dots them-selves.

· ·   · ·   · ·

Actually, of course, there is no such thing as a pair present. The pairness is something we contribute in organizing the dots as we look at them. We are so used to this problem of organizing things for ourselves that we forget that it hap-pens, but unless we remember it we won't be able to under-stand the way other people see the world or why they see it the way they do. Many puzzle problems are based on this principle. For instance, there is the story that a man stood on a bridge looking at some ducks swimming under him. There were two ducks in front, two in the middle, and two behind. The question is, "How many ducks were there?" The answer is clearly, "Six." Actually there were only four, as shown on page 54. The description of the situation was ambiguous. It did not supply enough information for us to answer the question, "How many ducks were there?" How-ever, we are used to dealing with an environment which does not supply enough information, so we add our own organization to the problem and, in this case, get the wrong answer.

Similarly, there are many cases where the environment provides two equally good "things" for us to see. On page 55 is one classic example of such an ambiguous picture. It can be seen either as a pair of faces almost kissing or as a kind of goblet. The picture itself does not determine which will be seen. Here it makes relatively little difference which we see. However, if we were rewarded every time we saw a goblet it would be very important to us. In a more complex situation, a factory itself can be just an ambiguous thing to look at. To one man it may be seen as a steppingstone to

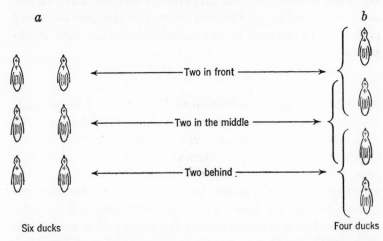

a   b

←———— Two in front ————→

←———— Two in the middle ————→

←———— Two behind ————→

Six ducks   Four ducks

something in his future. To another it may be a distasteful place in which he has to spend eight hours a day. The kinds of things it means to him will have a great deal to do with the way he behaves with respect to it, with the kinds of rewards he seeks from it, and with the kinds of rewards he finds in it. To understand his behavior, we must understand his view of the world.

Sometimes even at the simple level, the principles of organization do not help us very much in orienting our behavior with respect to the environment. Often when we look at a picture, the "figure" that stands out is what is supposed to be the "ground," and vice versa, and the thing doesn't make sense at all, or the good continuation of lines obscures what we are supposed to see, as in the case in puzzle pictures in which one is told to find five faces in the outlines of the leaves of a tree in a picture. In many cases we see even the simplest things in such a way that we cannot solve our problems, but usually at this level our organization is quite dependable and satisfactory. However, we have to go on, as we grow up, to much more complex organizations of the environment, and our difficulties begin to increase. Not only do we have to distinguish things from not-things, and people from things, but we have to distinguish friendly people from hostile people, and the like.

Earlier in this chapter we considered the things that motivate behavior. Everyone is constantly looking for various kinds of need-satisfactions. In this process we must decide which people and things are goals and which are not, which people and things are paths to goals and which are not, which paths have threatening characteristics as we go along them, which people and things are barriers to our success, and the like. All these things must be woven into a coherent organization that will guide our behavior. Because of the complexity of the environment, this is a difficult job. Its difficulty is enormously increased by the fact that conditions and people and things are always changing, so that our organizations must always be reshaped and modified to fit the new developments.

Because of the fact that the environment provides only ambiguous clues, we find that people are constantly shaping and reshaping their pictures of the world, and that from person to person there may be a great difference in what they see "outside" and the way they see it. Since all our behavior is directed toward the attainment of goals, it follows that our reorganizations of the world are attempts to find an organization that will lead us to considerably successful paths to goals. Everyone has such different goals from time to time, and such different experiences with the world around him, that we are apt to find great differences in the way in which the environment is organized by different people. Their behavior differs on this account, because the behavior is a function of the way the person sees things, and one of our commonest mistakes in understanding people flows from this. We are quite apt to say, "I don't understand why he did this, or why he feels that way," when the difficulty is that we are trying to explain someone else's behavior on the basis of our own organization of the world. Often, if we would stop to understand the way in which he sees things, we would recognize that his actions followed perfectly clearly from his perceptions.

From these two facts—the fact that we must provide order in the environment, and the fact that our goal-directed behavior is dependent on our organization of the world—it is quite reasonable that a particular organization acquires an emotional value in itself, if it works, and that there is considerable reluctance to give it up. Our views of people and institutions and events are seldom completely correct, and consequently seldom predict perfectly what is going to happen. For one thing, the things in the world outside are too numerous and complex to be handled at once, and so we develop broad oversimplified categories to handle them. Often these are partially correct and direct our behavior toward goals successfully in a large percentage of the cases. When this happens, the organization itself provides a security for us in leading us to goals, and for this reason, it takes on an emotional value of its own. When the environment presents evidence which is in conflict with our organization, we tend to reject the contradictory evidence to protect our categories, and there is a strong and emotional resistance to giving them up. It is no wonder that this process of changing one's mind is charged with emotion, when we consider the difficulties and uncertainties that are overcome by even a partially successful organization. Nor is it any wonder that we all shy away from rejecting an organization that has worked to some extent, for fear it may be exchanged for another period of anxiety-ridden uncertainty about what the goals and the paths really are.

As we shall see later on (Chapter 4), these organizations become real problems in our communication and thinking. We tend to see and hear well-organized wholes. We add the organization. Often the organization we add distorts the facts or makes it impossible to solve the problem. For example, consider the following problem in legal reasoning:

A passenger plane took off from country A en route for country C. It had to fly over country B to get there. During the trip it crashed exactly on the border of countries B and C. The legal problem that arose was where to bury the survivors. Should they be buried in country A where they came from or country C where they were going? Or should they, perhaps, be buried in country B, over which they had just passed. All the passengers were nationals of a fourth country, D.

Did you have an answer? Did you notice the problem? The answer, of course, is that one shouldn't bury the survivors at all—only those who didn't survive. But probably you were so set for a problem that you went right over the word and accepted the problem. Ask your friends this problem.

Generally the communication is so determined by the organization that they will tend to give you an answer about where to bury the survivors.

In addition to these internal organizational factors in perception, some other things influence the way we see things. One of them is the pressure of the group. For example, if you sit in a darkened room and look at a small point of light, it will eventually seem to move and wander erratically around the room. If a group watches this phenomenon and everyone reports where the light goes, what the group sees will influence what the individual sees. Not just what he *says* he sees, but what he actually sees. In another experiment, a group was asked to judge the relative length of two lines. A was clearly shorter than B. Each member of the group was asked to give his judgment in turn. The first man said "A longer," the second man the same, and so on. The first six were stooges, instructed to misreport what they saw. The question was what effect this would have on the seventh, who heard all the judgments. He often said "A longer." Subsequent interviews showed that in many cases he actually *saw* it as longer. In an even more frightening variation, groups were asked to say whether they agreed or disagreed with statements like "Honesty is the best policy" or "A dictator wouldn't be a good thing for our country." Previous tests showed they agreed. However, when, as in the preceding case, the group members each said "Disagree," many in the final position said, and actually felt, "Disagree." These influences on organization—internal from the stimulus or from motivation and external from the group—influence our perception, our thinking, and our attitudes.

These problems in the difficulty of achieving successful organizations of the world and the emotional charge that they acquire to resist change give rise to many of our everyday problems in communications and to much of the reluctance to adopt new methods that we see around us. In many of these cases, we would be well advised to look for the particular organization that causes the behavior that is objectionable, the attitude that stops communication, or the organization that is being protected by resistance to change, rather than assigning the blame to the kind of people we are dealing with. Often, a more adequate understanding of the way the other person sees the situation will enable us to present the facts or suggest the change in such a way that it is no longer threatening, and the difficulty will largely disappear. The problem may not lie in the person who is resistant, but in the way the material is presented to him.

SUMMARY

1. Behavior which seems to lead to reward tends to be repeated, and behavior which seems not to lead to reward, or to lead to punishment, tends not to be repeated.

2. All behavior is directed toward the satisfaction of needs, and there are at least three kinds of needs: (1) physical needs, (2) needs whose primary aim is in certain relationships with other people (social needs), and (3) needs whose primary aim is in a certain view of ourselves (egoistic needs). Unless we are careful of the manipulation of these needs, we are apt to find them conflicting with one another in the industrial situation. In addition, we have seen something of the structure of the needs with respect to one another, and something of what they mean in terms of their origin. The needs are divided into primary and secondary, and they are not substitutable one for the other, but the possibility of secondary needs depends partly on the satisfaction of primary needs. Further, as we see the social and egoistic needs in terms of their development from an attempt to guarantee satisfaction of physical needs, we can see something of the meaning of dependence and independence and something of the relation of the individual to other people.

3. The environment presents an ambiguous stimulus. We

must make sense of the environment in order to strive for the attainment of goals. All behavior is based on the world as it is seen by the behaving individual, and each of us becomes emotionally attached to his organizations of the world and is reluctant to give them up.

CHAPTER 3

LEADERSHIP AND SUPERVISION

As we begin to inquire into the problem of supervision, it is helpful to reexamine the nature of the leader's job—to look again at the relationship between the superior and the subordinate. Most of us have looked up from below at superiors' positions for many years and have seen in them chiefly more status and prestige, more power, more money, a bigger desk, and more telephones. Sometimes even when we move into higher jobs, these are still the outstanding characteristics in our minds. In order to be able to use some of the psychological principles from the last section, let us try to state the defining characteristics of the superior's role.

The nature of the superior-subordinate relationship

The superior is in a superior position because he is responsible for more work than one man can do. That is why he has subordinates. The fact that he has subordinates is the mark

61

by which we know he is in a superior position. The principal defining characteristic of his job is as simple as that. He is responsible for more work than he can do alone; therefore, he has subordinates to help him get it done. The successful accomplishment of the superior's job depends primarily on his ability to get help from his subordinates in getting the job done.

This means that the superior's job—at any level of the management hierarchy—is people, not production. He may be responsible for production, but the medium through which he accomplishes it is people, and his success or lack of it depends chiefly on his ability to work through people. Only at the level of the hourly paid worker, at the bottom of the organization chart, do we find people whose job is production. At any step of management above this—from the first level of supervision up to the top—the job is to accomplish production through the intervening medium of the subordinates who are there because the superior is responsible for more production than he can accomplish by himself. To be sure, at various levels of management the superior may have to worry about production schedules, distribution of products, the flow of materials, and the like, but he cannot *do* the production. He must create a situation such that his subordinates will help him accomplish his objective by actually achieving the production. If he gets this help from his subordinates he is a successful superior; if he does not get this help he is failing, in some degree, in his job.

It is not at all uncommon for members of line management, particularly above the middle levels of management, to say at this point, "I think all this business about human relations is very important in industry today. I wish I had more time to spend on it myself. Unfortunately, however, my main job is production, and I just can't give any time to human relations. We have a good man over in the Personnel Department, though, and we've made it his sole responsibility to check up on our human relations." This is not an unusual point of view. It is also quite easy to understand why a man would hold it. However, if our analysis is correct and the superior's main job is to create a situation such that his subordinates will help him get the job done, it is a completely mistaken point of view, and often a very expensive one. If we see the superior's job as one of accomplishing production through people, then it is the people, not the production, that must be his first consideration. He must watch the production and regulate it, because it is the thing on which the business organization succeeds or fails, but his primary effort must be directed toward the people who are going to accomplish production. The superior needs to worry first about handling his subordinates in such a way that they will help him get his job done. Then he can look at the production record. It will tell him whether or not he has done a good job as a superior. If he has created conditions such that his subordinates are helping him, the production will be high—disregarding, for the moment, interruptions in the flow of raw materials, machine breakdowns, and such external factors. If the production record is low, he should examine closely the techniques he has been using in dealing with subordinates.

It is not hard to understand why managers shun this point of view. It is much easier to think, as was suggested in the hypothetical quotation above, that one's job is production rather than human relations—that one's main responsibility is things rather than people. It is not particularly difficult to accomplish production when it is our own immediate job. If we are assembling widgets, we usually know just what to do and we have all the parts there to do it with. However, at the next step up the hierarchy the job is very different. Now, although the superior is responsible for the number of widgets turned out, he can't assemble them himself. He must accomplish the production through a very uncertain medium that intervenes between him and the widgets themselves—the people on the production line. It is a medium that is changeable, unpredictable, and intractable. It is a little like trying to pick a cherry from the bottom of a tall glass with two wobbly straws. It is easy to see what you are trying to do, but the instrument with which you are working is very hard to control. In many cases it seems likely that it is because of the difficulty of the medium through which production must be accomplished that managers turn away from the medium itself, in an unconscious effort to escape the problem, and say, "My job is production—I'll hire an expert staff man to worry about the people." Unfortunately, it seems to rest squarely in the nature of the relationship between superior and subordinate that human relations—worrying about people—is necessarily a line function and cannot be turned over to the staff.

In many cases, as organizations get large and complex, various levels of management are so far away from the actual production that they lose sight of the fact that their relationship with the basic production effort is through the people under them. As we move several steps up the family tree of the organization chart, it is still true that the superior has subordinates because he is responsible for more work than he can do himself. Now he has many subordinates, and they in turn have subordinates. Still, however, his successful execution of his job will depend on whether he can create conditions such that his subordinates help him to get the job done by creating conditions such that their subordinates help to get the job done, and so on down to the bottom of the chart. Now, instead of using two wet straws to pick up the cherry, the manager is in the nightmarish situation of having a chain of straws, one stuck in the end of the other, with which he must retrieve the cherry, and all of them wavering and giving way independently. His job is to stiffen them and make a useful instrument out of them. Little wonder, then, that he often tends to turn away from the crucial problem of the intervening medium—the straws—and maintains (wrongly) that his main job is production. It is much easier (though not so successful) that way. However, let us see whether we cannot find, in the psychological principles that have gone before, some guiding principles that will make it easier to do the job correctly.

The problem of dependence at work

What can we say, on the basis of our study of the nature of people in Chapter 2, that will help the supervisor to create conditions such that his subordinates will help him to get the job done? One of the things which we looked at, and which must be reexamined here, is the balance between dependence and independence in the development of the personality. We saw that the infant is born into the world with a set of needs to be satisfied, but without the means for satisfying them; he is dependent in the nature of the case. However, in the interests of insuring his survival, he must, in addition to allying himself firmly to the agents who satisfy his needs to guarantee their cooperation, develop an independent control over the means for his own need-satisfaction. Thus, in the early development of each of us, there comes a certain balance between the simultaneously existing contradictory characteristics of dependence and independence. As was pointed out before, the same thing is true at work. When a man first enters his job, he is chiefly dependent on his superiors at work for his need-satisfactions. By and large they control the things he must have. They control the rate of his pay, the continuance of his employment, and the physical conditions of his work on the one hand, and, on the other, the opportunities for social need-satisfaction (relationships with others, membership in the group, and the like) and egoistic need-satisfaction (opportunities for a feeling of being necessary on the job, for recognition of accomplishment, for growth and advancement). To a large extent, the subordinate is in the same position as the infant. He is dependent, and it is on the basis of this dependency that the superior gets his power to control the subordinate's behavior. However, if the superior chiefly exploits the dependency, we have the passively acquiescent yes man who does what he is told but does nothing else. If we are to utilize our subordinates maximally, we must provide opportunities for the development of active independence on the job so that we may have from them some of the initiative, self-directed effort, and growth of which they are capable. One of the superior's tasks is to achieve in his subordinates a productive balance of these two tendencies. The ways he does it are the techniques of leadership and the first steps in accomplishing his job of achieving production through the intervening medium of other people.

What can the superior do, specifically, to attain this balance? To answer this question, let me sketch briefly a set of possibilities that have been outlined more fully elsewhere by Douglas McGregor. McGregor points out that the superior's job is to create a situation such that the dependence which is necessarily present is as easy for the subordinate to bear as possible—such that the dependence does not threaten him unduly or stifle his initiative and activity. Once this is accomplished, the leader can go on to create conditions which will lead to a development of active independence in the subordinate, so that he may be a fully useful member of the work group. Three specific things are suggested under each of these main branches of the manager's job, and it seems worthwhile to go into each of them in a little detail.

Techniques of leadership

In the first place, under the heading of making the dependency as easy to live with as possible, it is suggested that *the superior must provide certain kinds of knowledge for the subordinate.* If we think back to the last chapter, we will remember that one of the basic psychological characteristics of people is that they have a problem in making sense out of the environment. It is a problem whose solution has great emotional importance to the individual. In the work situation, the subordinate comes to the job looking for various kinds of need-satisfactions, but uncertain about which patterns of behavior on his part and which people will lead him to success. He does not know, or knows only partly, the values in the situation, the rules according to which it operates (and according to which he is expected to operate), and the limits within which he has freedom to move. He must learn these; he must put the environment together to make sense out of it, so that he may securely take action in various directions toward the accomplishment of need-satisfactions. If the shape of his environment is not clear, if the values and rules and limits are not clear, he does not know how to proceed, and he is in an anxiety-producing situation, where it is clear that he is dependent on another for his success, but it is not clear what paths of action the other will approve as leading to the goal. It is because of this problem that it is especially important to provide certain kinds of knowledge to the subordinate.

It is a truism in industrial practice to say that we must tell a man what the company policies are, and the rules and regulations, that we must tell him what is expected of him, and what tools and resources are available to him to do it with. In many cases we are even going on beyond this point to insist that we must provide him with information about how well he is doing, so that he can check his hypotheses about the way the situation works. All these things are important; they are some of the kinds of information that must be provided to the subordinate so that he will not be lost in an uncertain and shifting morass in trying to make sense of his job. There are many other kinds of knowledge, however, that must be given to the subordinate, and one in particular is so apt to be withheld that it is worth individual attention.

The subordinate must know a good deal about the superior as a person. It is the superior himself who makes the other kinds of knowledge make sense. The rules do not mean anything except in terms of the superior as an individual. The rule book says that everyone must be at work at 8:00. Now the question arises, "How late is late?" The answer to this question is not to be found in the rule book, but in the superior. Late is when the boss thinks it is late. Is he the kind of man who thinks 8:00 is the time, and 8:01 is late? Does he think that 8:15 is all right occasionally if it is not a regular thing? Does he think that everyone should be allowed a 5-minute grace after 8:00 but after that they are late? The subordinate may be told what is expected of him, but the superior is the final judge who decides whether to interpret the level strictly or leniently. The subordinate must know the superior in this respect. The company handbook may say, "We encourage suggestions," but the subordinate must find out whether the superior is, in fact, the kind of person who wants suggestions to go up from his department, or whether he is afraid that would cast doubt on the supervision because he didn't think of them himself. All these things he must come to know about the superior. The superior can make it difficult or easy to learn them, and in many cases superiors seem to slip without thinking into a pattern of making it difficult for subordinates to "know" them.

There are two widespread beliefs, one of them unspoken and one explicit, which seem to work in the direction of making the superior hide himself as a person from his subordinates. In the first place, there seems to be a universal human tendency to hide and protect our personalities from others, because, in a certain sense, for another to "know" us gives him power over us. The superior remains aloof and depersonalized often because he feels that he must do so to retain power, and that to allow the subordinate to know him would be to relinquish some of this power. This is perhaps part of the reason why superiors call subordinates by their given names (a rather personal handle of the individual), while subordinates use depersonalized titles or "Mr." It is also akin to the fear, among certain peoples, of letting a photograph be taken, lest the likeness (and hence part of one's self) come into the hands of someone who would then have power over them. Whatever the nature, this unspoken belief seems to make superiors hold aloof from subordinates, as does the more common and more explicit prohibition against fraternizing with subordinates, and the explicit belief that familiarity breeds contempt. In this case, it seems clear that the evil root of fraternization lies not so much in the fact that the subordinate knows the personality of the superior, but rather in the fact that the superior will be suspected of favoritism and thus damage various aspects of group functioning. However, it seems quite possible for the superior both to avoid the arguments against letting himself be known and to provide the subordinate with the kind of knowledge that is essential for the subordinate to make sense out of the rule and expectations, without either giving the subordinate power over the superior or putting the superior in a position of singling out one of the group as a favorite.

There are other kinds of knowledge that sometimes fail to get communicated from the superior to his subordinate. We spoke, in an earlier chapter, about the situation that often arises where the superior hoards knowledge and thereby gains egoistic need-satisfactions. If he keeps information to himself, it seems to set him off as a man "in the know"; it may also make it more difficult for his subordinate to do his job. Often, also, the superior keeps back information simply by failing to make the reason for his decisions and policies explicit and clear when they should be. The reasons for his decisions may be a great help to his subordinates in doing their own work, but the superior may never have provided them with this information. An example in the experimental modification of a production line will illustrate the point. In an assembly job, girls typically brought their work to the foreman, asking him if it were defective or not. The foreman studied the assembly, and said either "No, that's all right," or "That one won't do—better throw it out." These seem like straightforward operations in the decision-making part of the foreman's job. However, later the line was changed so that each of the operators assembled the completed product, without a production-line organization. This meant that, to some extent, they took over the inspection function, since they had to decide on each completed piece whether it was acceptable or not. Although we might expect this new organization to be psychologically better in that it gave the girls a view of the over-all job and a better idea of their role in making the product, in fact it was impossible to continue the new system. The girls soon realized that they did not have standards on which to judge rejects. The foreman had always made the decision for them, without making the reasons for making the decisions explicit, and when the girls were put on their own they were completely incapable of deciding which pieces were unacceptable. If the foreman had gone one step further in the communication of information about the limits of the situation, he could have helped them to learn with each piece they brought him, by saying, for instance, "No, this one won't do; see, here the coupling isn't tight, and this is essential," or "This one is O.K. even though the neck isn't straight; that doesn't matter on this part," and the like. Part of what the subordinate has to learn is where the limits of the situation are. Every contact with the superior provides an opportunity for him to train his subordinate; he needs to be especially sensitive to these opportunities to provide knowledge to his subordinates and thereby to train them so that they can help him to get the job done.

A second important principle for the superior to observe in his attempt to make the subordinate's dependence as bearable as possible is less tangible than the first. He must *maintain an atmosphere of approval* at work. It is very hard to put into words just what is implied by this heading, but most of us can think of situations in which we have worked which were characterized by either the conspicuous presence or absence of an atmosphere of approval. Most of us have worked, at one time or another, in a situation where the superior held a particularly tight rein over things, seemed to be constantly looking for someone to do something wrong, and when he found a mistake, managed to give the impression that that was just about what he had expected all along. On the other hand, we have probably all also been in situations where we felt comparatively free and unhampered and able to operate with our whole selves in trying to do the job as we saw it. The difference between these two is largely a difference in the atmosphere of approval. While it is difficult to define it, it is not particularly difficult to sense it, as you go from group to group. Quite quickly one can sense, in a work group on the production floor, or in an office force, a tense fearful manner on the one hand, working in the fear of being caught doing something wrong, or on the other hand, a relaxed and easy atmosphere where the person feels free to try.

A good part of the atmosphere of approval is in the freedom to make mistakes. This does not at all mean tolerating lower standards of quality at work, but simply the recognition of an honest mistake that comes from someone's trying something and failing to accomplish it for various reasons. It is quite possible to point out mistakes to a subordinate and to correct them with an atmosphere of approval; it is quite possible to maintain a high quality of work performance and still give the subordinate a feeling of having freedom to make mistakes. Nor does an atmosphere of approval suggest a lowered standard of rate of output. The two do not necessarily go together at all. It is quite possible to hold high standards of quality and quantity with an atmosphere of approval, and it is equally possible to have rather low standards in an atmosphere of disapproval. The chief difference will be in the subordinate's feeling about himself, his job, and his boss, and consequently a difference in his effectiveness at work.

An interesting example of the atmosphere of approval and the freedom to make mistakes appears in a study of supervision on the C. and O. Railroad made by the Survey Research Center of the University of Michigan. In *Productivity, Supervision, and Morale,* they report the following: Two groups of section gangs had been distinguished on the basis of their productivity. One group was characterized by consistent high productivity and the other by consistent low productivity. Both groups were asked, "What does the foreman do when you do a bad job?" The answers were separated into those which did not carry an atmosphere of approval (such as "bawl you out") and those suggesting correction with an atmosphere of approval (such as "shows you how to do it right" or "just tells you about it"). The foremen of the high-production work groups characteristically used the latter method—that is, their correction of mistakes carried an atmosphere of approval. The relation between leadership techniques and productivity is something which we shall have to examine in more detail later on.

Still another example of the effect of an atmosphere of approval is found in the same set of studies of productivity. The researchers examined the techniques of supervision of a group of foremen whose work force had high-production records and the techniques of foremen whose groups had low-production records. They discovered that the foremen who could be described as "production-oriented" had lower production records than those who were described as "employee-oriented." This means that the superior who is continually watching production records, and waiting for the subordinate to fail to accomplish something, actually limits production by creating an atmosphere where the subordinate cannot work effectively. On the other hand, the foremen who primarily attended to their subordinates and concentrated on making it possible for them to do their jobs in fact accomplished more production.

The third thing the superior can do to make it easier for the subordinate to operate in a dependent situation is to *maintain consistent discipline.* If we go back for a moment to some of the principles in Chapter 2, we see the importance of this consistency. One of the problems that all people have is to make sense of an environment that is vague, ambiguous, and confusing. Each person has to learn, little by little, what the main shape of the situation is, what the rules are, where the limits are, and what actions are approved and disapproved in this particular part of the world. If the rules are not consistent, and if the limits won't hold still, it is impossible to learn about the situation, and the person is in a very difficult position of having to work in an environment about which he cannot feel sure or secure. He may or may not know how to get ahead, or to protect himself in it. To help him we must provide clues to the organization of the environment which are as consistent as possible. Often we do not point out an infringement with the feeling, "Well, I'll let it go this time; it's a little thing, and there's no point in hounding him about it." This is usually accompanied by the feeling that we have been lenient and actually done a favor to the violator in overlooking the infringement. How-

ever, the fact of the matter is that we are treating ourselves
to a favor by avoiding the correction when we are not sure
how well we can administer it, and it is done at the expense
of the subordinate, who is now not sure whether this is an
infringement or not. In his view it has seemed to be the
rule in the past, but, after all, it wasn't called this time.
Maybe this particular superior doesn't hold to this particular
rule. A situation of this sort can generate a great deal of
insecurity and anxiety and leave the subordinate completely
in the dark about what to do and what not to do. It would
actually be more of a favor to the subordinate to call each
infringement closely and consistently. He will not feel
"hounded" if it is done with an atmosphere of approval. He
will, though, grow more secure in the feeling that he knows
exactly where the limits of the situation are.

All of us must feel some of this insecurity as a result of
inconsistent discipline in various everyday situations. One
of the commonest is in our relations with traffic policemen.
In many ways the relation between motorists and policemen
parallels that between the subordinate and superior very
closely. In each case, the one is almost completely dependent on the other, who interprets the rules (within limits),
administers rewards and punishments, and has almost complete say in the situation. Whenever we are speeding on the
highway, we must feel some of this same sort of anxiety.
After all, we are breaking the written rule; on the other
hand, it often isn't enforced. Maybe this is a place, or a
set of policemen who don't take the rule seriously, and we
can speed a little. But still there is the lurking insecurity,
because he may, at any time, decide to enforce this particular rule. Can we park in a no-parking zone? It says not,
but often it is not enforced, and a lot of other people are
getting away with it. All of us must feel, from time to time,
that it would be a lot easier to operate in the situation if
they would just be consistent about it one way or the other.

We can also remember the principle of the Law of Effect from Chapter 2, according to which that behavior which seems to lead to reward tends to be repeated, while that behavior which seems to lead to punishment tends to be eliminated. By the use of this principle the superior shapes his work force, to produce the kind of behavior that is necessary on the job. The rules and standards are set up on the job to define the kind of behavior that is essential. Unless these rules and standards are consistently enforced, the Law of Effect has no chance to operate to produce the desired behavior on the part of the work group, and the superior has failed to show his subordinates what he expects of them. Usually the failure to maintain consistency is due to the fact that the superior is reluctant to administer discipline. When this happens the superior is indulging himself in a luxury of not doing his job because it is difficult and distasteful. He must allow himself some leeway in this matter, but he must also do a kind of cost accounting to see how much this luxury is costing him in terms of its effect in not producing the kind of behavior in his subordinates that is necessary to help him get the job done.

Once the superior has created conditions—through providing knowledge, consistency, and approval—such that the subordinate is not hampered by his feelings of dependency, he can turn to the attempt to provide opportunities for active independence, so that he may have a subordinate with initiative, and so that he may take advantage of the subordinate's interests and abilities. McGregor points out a similar set of techniques for fostering independence in employees, so that a more constructive kind of cooperation can be obtained.

The first of these is to *provide opportunities for growth* and expansion of the individual's social and egoistic need-satisfactions. If the individual is to grow in independence, he must come to feel that he *is* something, that he is a member of the group, that he can do something, and that he is important to the task and to the group. It is the leader's job to be on the lookout for opportunities to foster the development of such feelings. They include not only the opportunities for actual advancement in pay, position, and responsibility, though these are important, but also the learning of new skills, a feeling of one's role in the total productive effort, a feeling that one is personally responsible for the accomplishment of certain functions, and that these functions are essential to the completed whole. To whatever extent it is possible, the individual should be helped to see that he is uniquely responsible and required on the job, and that he is an integral member of the group in a social as well as a productive sense. These are among the important social and egoistic need-satisfactions that are available on the job, and it is essential that the superior utilize them in providing on-the-job returns to the subordinate so that he may be maximally useful to himself and to the organization.

In discussing the various kinds of need-satisfaction in Chapter 2, we raised the question of why, in many cases, employees worked indifferently on the job and painstakingly and long at a hobby at home, or why the boss so often seems to have a different attitude toward his work from that of his employees. Much of the difference seems to lie in the fact that the job provides too little social and egoistic need-satisfaction for the employee. It does not involve his whole person or his whole ego. His product is not his own, and he feels no particular pride in accomplishment from it, but only a step toward his pay check. Unless the job is more to him, he will never be able to give it the other kind of interest. This problem becomes particularly acute when it is coupled with the deskilling of jobs that is the inevitable concomitant of technological change and production-line methods. As the individual craftsman disappears it becomes harder for a workman to feel that he, himself, is essential on the job. As we build jobs so that it will take a minimum of training to fill them, and so that a man may be replaced with a minimum of dislocation to production, we automatically build jobs which minimize the feeling of individual contribution to the product. It becomes harder and harder for the individual to feel that *his* skills and know-how are required. Unless we can be constantly alert for opportunities to help him to see that he is, in fact, an essential part, we must be content to accept his merely partial involvement in the job, and a lackadaisical walking through the job.

It seems quite possible that the superior's greatest opportunity to control absenteeism and turnover also lies in this same area of being alert to opportunities to provide his subordinates with a feeling of growth and expansion of social and egoistic need-satisfactions. Many of the causes of absenteeism and turnover are beyond our control. A broken leg or a serious illness is going to lead to absence no matter what the superior does. However, the cases over which we can hope to exercise control are those in which the subordinate is in doubt about whether he is really sick enough not to be able to come to work. If his job is one about which he feels no personal involvement, and in which he feels that he is easily and immediately replaceable, there is no great push to come to work. If, however, the employee feels himself to be a member of the group, feels his own skills and understanding to be essential, and feels himself to be part of the job, those feelings will be quite likely to swing the balance and bring him to work. The employee's feeling about himself and his relation to the job and the group are largely the superior's responsibility. He must be awake to the opportunities to provide expanding need-satisfactions for subordinates.

The second leadership technique that might be suggested for the development of active independence is that of *securing the subordinate's participation* in all possible aspects of the job. It is very difficult to overemphasize the importance of participating from a psychological point of view. Time after time, in industrial studies, research workers have come back to participation as a basic principle by which a subordinate may be given an opportunity to develop, his morale may be improved, and his skills and abilities may be maximally and productively utilized. At first glance, there does not seem to be much room for participation in supervision, but as we look at jobs around us a host of possibilities arises.

There is often an initial resistance to participation, on the basis of the fear that it will leave the superior without the customary prerogatives of management. This is not necessarily true, however, for there are many areas in which it is possible to elicit and encourage participation without giving up any of the traditional unilaterality of decisions. There are many decisions—about the placing of desks or tools, about staggering relief periods, about social activities, and the like —that can be kept completely outside the normal prerogatives. There is no doubt, however, that they may lead to participation which does encroach on things that have traditionally been seen as management's prerogatives, in that the subordinate may want to participate in decisions that have previously been solely in management's bailiwick. It can only be said that such encroachments are controllable, and further, that it may well be found that it is quite profitable to give up some of the privacy that management has had in its prerogatives in the interests of gaining more productive efficiency as the fruit of the subordinate's participation.

Participation has the unique characteristic of giving a person a chance to *be* a part of the final process, and a chance to expand and develop as a participant, as well as providing an opportunity for him to contribute to the final outcome. On both these counts—because of the different relation of the man to the job as well as his greater contribution to the job—participation is one of the most useful leadership techniques. It should be added, however, that it must be a real participation and not a sham. In many cases superiors invite participation only after they know the answer, with the idea that it would be good for the men to "have a feeling" of participating. Nothing is more apt to be sensed by the participant than the fact that he isn't taken seriously and that his participation is not real. It is apt to produce a great deal more of a liability for him to feel duped than it would have to be left unconsulted. If a superior is going to invite participation he must be ready to take it seriously and be swayed by it, as well as ready for it to open many areas that he hadn't anticipated. If this is not possible, he would do better to avoid it in the first place.

Industrial suggestion systems are a form of participation, and they often seem to break down for just such a reason. Usually the work group is invited to make suggestions, but they do not have sufficient information about the crucial problems to make penetrating suggestions. The way has not been paved for participation. The result is that the suggestions are superficial and peripheral. Superiors then take a patronizing air toward the suggestions because they are not answers to the questions that they (the superiors) saw, even though little effort was made to make these questions universally understood among the work group. The next step is a decision to "give him $5 for trying, and to encourage him," and soon the whole plant senses the phoniness of the suggestion system. Real participation can pay real dividends; we have ample evidence in industrial practice to show it. Fake participation is apt to be more of a liability than an asset.

It is difficult to overestimate the effectiveness of participation. It appears in very many situations in surprising form. An experiment was done during the war in an attempt to change food habits, so that meat would be more efficiently used during a shortage. Groups of housewives were gathered to try to get them to use more of the less desirable parts of food animals—the heart, brains, kidneys, etc. A skilled nutritionist talked to the group for an hour about the nutritional value of these parts, about how to prepare them, and the like, and a follow-up study was made to see how many of the women served the foods. Only 3 per cent had tried them—a discouraging result! In other groups, a discussion leader, who knew nothing about nutrition or cooking, but who was skilled in eliciting participation, got the women to discuss the problems themselves and spent the same amount of time as the lecturer. Another follow-up study was made, and now 32 per cent of the women had tried the previously nonpreferred foods—a striking effect of the group decision in changing behavior. Other experiments have indicated, for instance, that if one asks a group of people to write down their childhood memories, a very large proportion of the things they remember will be things in which they participated. More than any of the big things that may have happened outside of them, people tend to remember things of which they themselves were a part. If we are trying to disseminate a company policy, it might be well to consider this finding concerning the degree to which it may be recalled, and the food-preference study in terms of the degree to which lecturing and participation may change behavior.

Still another example of participation as a managerial technique is useful here. A food-processing company organized on a national basis has, by the nature of its product, a somewhat seasonal business. They have taken advantage of this to shut down all the plants during the lull, and bring all of management—especially the foremen—to a series of meetings on company problems. The subjects cover a wide variety of topics—operations, personnel, competition, and the like—and the participation in discussion includes almost everyone. The foremen will ask, "Why can't we use a No. 2

screen in our processing the way they do at———?" "Why
do we have a helper on———operation instead of a packer?"
"Why don't we pack———?" These meetings illustrate
clearly one of the key problems of participation: management is faced squarely with the necessity for stating its
policy in all areas, and either making the policy understandable or changing it. There is little room in this kind of session for a management that must say, "That's the way it's going to be because that's the way we set it up." Indeed, in
many of these meetings management has to say, "I don't
know the answer to that question; I'll get the facts together
and we'll give you an answer at the next meeting." The
outcome of a series of such meetings is bound to change
the relation between top management and the lower levels,
to clarify the policy and the lower levels of supervision's
relation to policy, and to engender a much more productive
feeling on the part of the foremen. Unfortunately, in this
case, it is not possible to present evidence, in the form of
production records, of the effect of these participation sessions. It is only possible to say that it is a very successful operation, and all the superficial signs indicate that the meetings have a very beneficial effect in making the first lines of
supervision truly members of the management organization.

It is interesting to speculate about the source of the very
powerful force that is associated with participation. It may
well be that much of the leverage that comes from participative techniques arises from the same kind of industrial
growth that we have discussed in other areas. With increasing growth of large industrial cities and the disappearance
of small communities, the individual is losing his membership in and participation in small primary groups. The routinization of large industry takes away part of his feeling of
belonging and of being necessary to the operation. The increase in size has gone along with a deterioration of participation in church groups, community groups, school groups,

and even with radical changes in the degree to which the family unit is a strong group in which the members participate fully. In the absence of these kinds of belongingnesses, it may well be that we have an unusual opportunity to provide, by industrial leadership, a kind of participation that is lacking elsewhere, which will fill a real need of the individual, and at the same time be a very useful tool in accomplishing the productive goals of the business.

The third suggestion in the interests of developing active independence is to provide a real *right of appeal*. There is no final escape from dependency if the superior is the ultimate authority, with no appeal beyond his interpretation or ruling. Unless there is some outside authority to which the subordinate can appeal, he never can be entirely safe in his dependency or quite able to develop a real independence. Moreover, like participation, the right of appeal must be a real right, and more than a formal right. We have progressed considerably with formal grievance mechanisms, but it does no good if the attitude says implicitly, "Sure, you can go over my head, but I'll never forget it if you do." An appeal over his head is bound to threaten anyone in a superior position. It is his function as a superior to permit the appeal in such a way that his own insecurity does not threaten his subordinate. He must make the right of appeal a real possibility, not a formal rule. The same thing is true of the superior's role with respect to participation. When a subordinate makes a suggestion, it may seem to carry an implication that if the superior were smart enough to deserve the superior position he would have thought of it himself. Such an implication, whether it is really in the subordinate's suggestion or only in the superior's mind, threatens the superior's own egoistic need-satisfactions and may well lead him to act in such a way that further participation is made difficult or impossible. In both participation and the right of appeal, the leader must realize the threat to his leadership role implicit in them and must handle himself in such a way that both continue to be real possibilities. It is perhaps worth noting, in this connection, that the grievance mechanism, which was introduced by the union in many industries, fills much of this need. It was pressed for, in many cases, because it was badly needed in particular plants, and this demand was one of the organizing cries of the union. It may well be that here the union has taken over and fulfilled a role which initially properly belonged to management but which management failed to fulfill.

In American industry today, one of the biggest tasks that confronts supervision is to help subordinates to find a real role for themselves as persons on the job. Two developments have led to making this an extremely critical area. In the first place, the deskilling and routinizing of jobs has greatly increased the number of people who can no longer feel that their peculiar combinations of skills and experience are necessary on the job. We are building jobs so that the individual is less attached to them as a person than before, and the superior must help to overcome this.

More importantly, however, this development is tending to provide a kind of return for work which splits the employee clearly and completely into two people: the worker, on the one hand, and the person on the other. As we look at the kinds of human needs discussed in Chapter 2, it will be noticed that there is a great difference between the physical need-satisfactions in one group and the social and egoistic need-satisfactions in another. We pay (in dollars and cents) primarily in physical need-satisfactions. They provide a form of reward that cannot be enjoyed on the job. By and large, our physical need-satisfactions must be utilized off the job, and they are accepted as a goal to be enjoyed at the end of work. The social and egoistic need-satisfactions can, in many cases, be provided and realized on the job itself, and they can serve to identify the individual as a person with the job, so that he feels part of it, and it of him. The job can then be partly a goal in itself, as well as a path to physical need-satisfactions beyond the job. This is the psychological situation that characterizes the craftsman; he is personally involved in his job, and commits all his interests and abilities to it. It is a far cry from the worker who sees his job as something that must be endured in order to get other satisfactions afterward. There seems to be no question but what the former situation is more productive, and there seems equally to be no question but what it is a great deal more satisfying to the individual as a person.

SUMMARY

1. The superior has subordinates because he is responsible for more work than he can do himself. Consequently his job is to get help from his subordinates. His job is people, not production. To do his job well, he must create conditions such that he gets help from his subordinates.

2. One of the outstanding problems in the subordinate's relationship to his superior is in the problem of the subordinate's dependence on the superior and on the need to alleviate the difficulty of this dependence and to make possible the development of an active independence to provide for constructive cooperation on the part of the subordinate.

3. To do this it is suggested that three things (among many others) help the subordinate to feel easy in his dependency: knowledge (of various sorts), an atmosphere of approval, and consistent discipline. Another set of three is suggested to foster the development of active independence: the encouragement of growth and expansion of egoistic and social need-satisfactions, participation, and the right to appeal.

4. Finally, it is suggested that one of the superior's chief opportunities to manage well lies in the area of developing social and egoistic need-satisfactions at work, so that the subordinate may be identified with his work as a person, not merely as a routinized robot waiting for his pay.

□□□□□□□□□□□□□□□□□□□□□□□□□
□
□
□   # COMMUNICATION
□
□
□
□
□
□
□
□

One of the major responsibilities of a leader is the establishment and utilization of a communication system. His communications with his subordinates are the medium through which he directs their efforts. By means of these communications the leader defines the goals of the organization and the subgroup; he tells the subordinate what is expected of him, what resources are available, how well he is doing, and the like. The communications from the superior are the things on the basis of which the subordinate is able to form a stable organization of his work world. They are the medium through which the superior can administer reward and punishment and, by a utilization of the Law of Effect, help the subordinate to learn what the boundaries of the situation are, and which behaviors are approved and which disapproved. Without a rich flow of communications from the superior, the subordinate cannot know what the

85

situation is, which direction he should be going, how well he is doing, and the like; without good communication he is in an impossibly insecure position.

On the other hand, the communication from the subordinate to the superior is a real necessity to the successful leader. It is on the basis of these communications that the superior knows his subordinates. It is on the basis of these communications that the superior can diagnose misperceptions on the part of his subordinates of the goals of the group, of their own role and what is expected of them, of their degree of success, and the like. Upward communications provide the first symptoms of tension and difficulties in the group as they reflect aggressions and insecurities. Further and perhaps most important, it is on the basis of these messages that the superior can see the role which he himself plays, can tell the way in which he is seen by his subordinates, and consequently can fashion his behavior accordingly. A sensitivity to the movement of communications is one of the prime requisites of a successful leader, and the utilization of communications both to and from the leader can be one of his greatest assets.

"Two-way" communication

So far, this description of the problem of communication sounds very much like the emphasis on so-called "two-way communications" which is one of the current fads of personnel philosophies. Indeed, to a certain extent it is just such an emphasis. However, the problem of communication is not nearly so simple. The problem of communication is not merely to provide an opportunity for person A to say something to B and for B to say something back to A. Each of them is concerned that the other not only hears what he says, but also accepts it, integrates it into his own view of the world, and acts on it, rather than distorting it, rejecting it, or hiding it away. As we get into the problem in more detail, we see many of the principles that were brought out in Chapter 2 playing a very important role in communication.

One of the easiest mistakes to make in the practice of communication is to feel that because we have heard ourselves say something, the other person necessarily has heard us say it too and, moreover, has heard much the same thing munication process probably usually go something like this: that we heard ourselves say. The steps in the normal com- Suddenly A thinks of something. He thinks, "I must tell B so-and-so." He goes over to B and says "So-and-so." At this point, A is quite apt to be through. He has put the idea in words. He has got it outside himself, and he has heard it out there, so he usually assumes that it has taken the next step —that is, that it has gone from being outside A to being inside B. Consequently A is quite apt to walk away confident in his communication. However, he may go further. He may ask B, "Do you get it?" or "Is that clear?" Now, by and large, these are questions to which B is only allowed to answer "Yes"; for B to say anything else suggests an inadequacy in him, so the answer is apt to be irrelevant to the communication. However, even if B is a strong character, and his "Yes" means actually "Yes, I do understand what you said," he still can only mean "I understand what I heard," not "I understand what you heard yourself say." If the communication is of any importance, A must have more information than this; he must know something of what B heard.

At first glance this seems to make the problem of communication almost impossible. On the one hand, we are apt to think that no serious misunderstanding will arise if A assumes that B heard A say the same thing that A heard himself say, and on the other hand, it seems very difficult for A ever to find out what B did hear, if he can't trust the answer when he asks B, "Did you understand that?" Indeed, it is

difficult to communicate. We are probably saved mostly by
the fact that there is a very great tolerance in the degree of
understanding that we require of one another; very little
precision is asked of most of our communications. However,
it is still possible for A to find out a good deal more about
what B heard. Even though he can't trust B's response when
he asks him directly, there are other techniques. If A, after
he has made his statement, simply does not walk away, and
does not ask any questions, but only stands a moment in an
expectant pause, he will create a situation in which B is
much more likely to tell him what he heard. B, feeling that
the matter is not closed, and that some sort of response is
required of him, will probably either ask questions, reveal-
ing his conception of the communication, or repeat the gist
of it, so that A now knows not only what he heard himself
say but, to some extent, what B heard.

Communication and the organization of the environment

If we think back for a moment to the discussion of the
organization of the environment in Chapter 2, we see that
the other problem—the fact that B may have heard A say
something different from what A heard himself say—is more
serious. Each individual has the problem of organizing a
sensible and coherent world for himself out of an external
environment which does not make sense in itself. The same
problem is present in communication. When A talks to B,
he never tells B everything. He relies on B to fill in gaps, to
relate the material to larger patterns, and to organize the
whole thing into a sensible order. In doing this B will very
often organize the material in such a way that the words no
longer mean the same thing to him that they did to A. A
little thought will probably call to mind instances in which
each of us spoke confidently about something, only to find
that our listener was interpreting a key word differently

and had distorted the whole thing completely. However, an example may show the point even better.

Immediately below, you will see a square made up of nine dots. The problem is to draw four straight lines which

·   ·   ·

·   ·   ·

·   ·   ·

join all nine dots. Try the problem yourself. Copy the dots on another piece of paper and see if you can do it. You are not allowed to lift your pencil from the paper, and every time you change the direction of a line (turning or retracing) it counts as another line. You are not allowed to fold the paper.

It usually seems very hard to do. Five lines would do it nicely, but four seems very difficult. However, it is not difficult at all. If you will look at the figure shown below, you will see how it can be done. It looks peculiar, but it is only four lines, and it does go through all the dots.

Almost everyone will try to solve the problem while staying inside the square of dots. Many people even say, "Oh, but you told me to stay in the square." Actually the instructions did not say that the lines must be in the square. In fact, there is no square there. The dots are an example of the

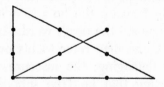

situation in which the environment provides an ambiguous stimulus, which the perceiver organizes into a square. Rather than see nine unconnected dots, we typically see them joined together in a good square, and this organization, which we provide, leads us to interpret the instructions in a particular way. It does not matter that the instructor heard himself clearly and knows that he did not say to stay within the square. To make sense of the environment, the problem solver will add his own instructions, and to make sure of the communication, the instructor should get some response back from the subject to indicate how this particular piece of the world is interpreted. Very nearly the same kind of thing happens at work when a subordinate is given part of the information on the superior's belief that the rest is unnecessary. The subordinate, being faced with the necessity of making sense out of many parts of his environment, will organize it as best he can, and often not in the manner intended.

Communication and motivation

This is an example of a situation in which principles of organization arising from factors within the outside environment dictated the kind of sense the observer would make of the world, in the manner indicated in Chapter 2. Other kinds of pressures act to determine particular organizations, too. Very often motivations and emotions tend to alter the way in which things are seen and heard, and these must be taken into account in assessing our communication. Industrial organizations are hierarchical, and what the boss says has meaning because the boss said it. His words are not just words; they are the boss's words. If he says "Things aren't going well," he may refer to his own feeling of inadequacy about managing; the insecure subordinate may hear him suggesting that he (the subordinate) is falling down on the job. If the boss says "Things are going to expand here soon," he may be referring to plans for new space and new machinery, and knowing the content of his own ideas, he clearly hears the reference. The ambitious sub-

ordinate, however, equally clearly hears a promise of possibilities of advancement, and if they are not forthcoming,
he will be resentful since he has had an explicit promise. In
all these cases, the motivations and emotions of the listener
and the kind of need systems to which he refers the statement determine its meaning. In order to avoid gross misunderstanding, it is essential for A to know not only what he
heard himself say but what B heard.

Such misunderstandings are not at all uncommon outside industry. During World War II, an aerial-gunnery student was taking a training flight over the Gulf of Mexico.
The pilot, enjoying the ride and the scenery, pointed over
the side of the plane, in a friendly spirit, to call the student's
attention to a speedboat below. The gesture was clear to
him, but the student referred it to his own acute terror of
being in the air, and interpreting it to mean that his worst
fears were realized, he parachuted over the side. In many
senses the two people were not acting in the same world,
and the pilot's attempt to communicate without fitting his
symbols to the world of the listener was typical of a very
common error in communication patterns.

Often the meaning of a fact may become, for various reasons, very special to one person or a group of people, and a
reference to it will elicit quite different responses in them
than in others. It is essential, in such cases, to realize this
fact, and to trim communication techniques to fit the organization of the listener. Before the war a company had nego-
tiated a certain rate for a particular job. When it became impossible to hire at that rate, they raised the pay without
changing the contract. The higher rate continued during the
war when it was hard to hire people, and there was sufficient turnover so that at the end of the war no one in the
job had ever been paid at the old (contracted) rate. When
applicants became more plentiful, the manager went back
to the old rate. The union objected, saying the rate had been

changed by practice. The manager protested that the contract was the same and the rate had not been changed. If he had been more careful to know the organization of the world which his subordinates had, and to know which media of communication were effective with them, he would have avoided a considerable strain on their relationship and a costly arbitration which he eventually lost.

These are not examples of cases where the individual deliberately and willfully chose to misinterpret information in line with his motives. Under the influence of a strong motive the facts may be distorted so that they actually look different to the person. When one gets up at night to investigate a strange sound and goes into the darkened living room, the coat thrown over a chair momentarily and temporarily actually is a terrifying figure, and it is responded to as such. It does not matter that another person may know that it is only a coat, or that the investigator himself may subsequently learn that it is only a coat. At the time of his misperception, under the influence of his motivation, the only thing that is real is his experience, and his experience covers a threatening figure rather than a discarded coat. The psychological environment may not agree entirely with what we know to be physically present, but what is psychologically present—molded by our fears and hopes as well as by other mechanisms—is the thing that determines our behavior.

Psychological mechanisms protecting organizations

There is still another characteristic of human beings, arising out of the individual's problem in organizing his environment, which acts to impede and distort communications. Once we have achieved a satisfactory organization of a piece of the world we tend to retain it, even in the face of contradictory information. Facing an ambiguous situation generates an acute anxiety in us. When the situation is one which has considerable importance to us—as when we must decide which paths of action will lead to success, or what philosophy of life or political point of view is best—the pressure is increased. It then becomes extremely important to us to bring some order into the facts and to achieve a stable organization on the basis of which our behavior may be directed. Once such an organization is achieved, we tend to retain it and protect it, rather than to admit other facts and let it change, because the possibility of change involves leaving the security of an existing organization that works.

Several techniques are common for this kind of protection of existing organizations. In the first place, we tend to select those sources of information which will present facts in harmony with our present pattern, and to avoid sources of information which do not fit easily with our organizations. Beyond this, if we are confronted with discrepant information, it is a characteristic of human mental process to distort the information, to reject or overlook it, to reinterpret it or explain it away, and as a final resort, to eliminate it gradually through selective forgetting. All these processes act to preserve and protect existing organized attitudes and pictures of the world, and whenever one aims to change such an attitude they must be taken into account. They are of sufficient importance to communication to warrant a more detailed examination.

One of the greatest difficulties in effecting a communication which will change our minds lies in the fact that we all tend to select sources of information which purvey material with which we already agree. This is not at all a deliberate conscious choice to bolster our own prejudices or to avoid seeing the other side of the question. Rather it is because the information from these sources tends to make sense to us, is understood easily, and is couched in the kinds of phrases we understand. All these things at once select the source for us and protect us from having to change our minds. The phenomenon is quite common in industry. When a group assembles to discuss the kinds of problems raised in this book, we find that the personnel men go to personnel meetings, the vice-presidents to vice-presidents' meetings, and the foremen to foremen's meetings. Each finds himself in a group where the others have the same general kinds of organization of the world that he has. As the meeting goes on, the personnel men say personnel kinds of things to one another, they hear their own points of view presented in different words, and they go away reinforced in their original opinions. Similarly with the others. This example is not meant to belittle personnel men or vice-presidents or foremen in particular. Rather it is a characteristic of all of us, and the tendency to choose sources of information which present facts in agreement with already existing organizations is one of the large barriers to communication designed to change a person's mind.

During the war the Treasury Department produced a movie about buying war bonds. It was one of a series of techniques directed toward changing people's behavior in this particular dimension—toward increasing bond purchases. A test was conducted to determine its effectiveness in changing people's minds and actions. A particular community was chosen for study, and a sample of the audience interviewed in detail to find out who went and what kind of effect the movie had had. Tickets to the movie had been distributed free through service clubs, women's clubs, religious groups, newspaper offices, and the like, so that they were available to almost everyone who might want to go. However, when the interviews were conducted it was found that the people who attended were those who were already giving blood at the blood banks and were already buying bonds. The movie had attracted the people who were already convinced. Those for whom participation in activities closely related to the war effort seemed important were attracted by the idea of the movie, and they chose to go to see the film urging them to participate. Those who did not participate in such activities were not interested in the film, and by and large did not go. Unfortunately this is the fate of many of our attempts to change people's minds. The people who already agree are the only ones who listen.

In many cases, however, all of us find ourselves confronted with facts which are at variance with our already existing view of the situation—facts which threaten our organization of the world. A simple selection of the media which carry facts to our liking is not enough. We cannot successfully avoid being faced with discrepant information. At this point, in order to protect existing organizations and to avoid the insecurity of ambiguity, there is a group of psychological mechanisms that act to reject and distort information in the interest of preserving a stable organization.

One of the things that we very often do is simply to overlook such incongruent facts. Most of us probably do this particularly in the cases of complicated problems and problems which are close to our personal values. Certainly there is a good deal of such overlooking or rejecting of information in connection with our assessment of the personalities of our families and our friends, and probably even more in the case of our own personalities. We think of ourselves as having certain sorts of characteristics, and even though we may act quite differently on occasion, these items are conveniently omitted from our picture because they do not fit. Similarly, on complicated issues it is often possible to overlook the relevance of various items of information which are at variance with our view of the situation.

To take another example from the wartime bond campaigns, a survey was conducted early in the war to determine why people bought war bonds. Most of them (65 per cent in April, 1943) said it was to finance the war; at this time 14 per cent said it was to help prevent inflation. A tremendous advertising campaign was conducted in the next few years, with the prevention of inflation an important theme. In June, 1945, 68 per cent of the people thought bonds should be bought to help finance the war and 14 per cent thought they should be bought to help prevent inflation. Certainly this is a very discouraging suggestion about the possibility of changing people's minds, even with a kind of publicity campaign that was virtually universal in its contact. After two years of this kind of publicity about the inflationary effect of a shortage of consumer goods and the increase in purchasing power, 54 per cent of the people either said that bond purchases had no effect on prices or said that they could not see any relation between the two. The disheartening suggestion is that the information about inflationary pressures was communicated to those who already realized them and the information about supporting the war reached those who already held this position. There is very little real evidence of any change in opinion.

In face-to-face communications, all of us have been in situations where people have been quite impervious to facts that were being presented. Indeed, in many arguments one often gets the impression that the "listener" is not, in fact, a listener at all. He is simply politely remaining silent until it is his turn to speak, meanwhile mustering his own arguments. His reply is apt to be almost totally irrelevant to the preceding speaker's statement. He often seems to have completely ignored the points. Such rejection obviously poses a real problem in communication and must be recognized if it is present.

More frequently, however, it is not possible to reject items completely. In these cases the tendency is to distort them so that they fit into the already existing organization. A fact is not complete by itself; it has meaning partly in terms of the context in which it is seen. Consequently, in many cases we find that a piece of information which has been intended by the speaker in a particular way is changed and remodeled by the hearer to fit another context. Indeed, when it is heard in the new context, there is no need to change it; the simple fact of its contextual relations will make the change. There is no question here of a deliberate and conscious attempt to distort, but only of a variation in meaning which comes from the interpretation given to a fact by including it in a particular context.

This kind of distortion is well illustrated in a series of experiments that have been done on the way in which people form impressions of a personality. If we were to ask people to describe the actions of someone who is "helpful, quick, and skillful" as opposed to another person who is "helpful, quick, and clumsy," the word "quick" which is in both descriptions means quite different things. In the first case it is the quickness of a person who is deft and sure and whose help is successful and welcome. In the second case the quickness is a blundering sort of rushing in where the helpfulness is more apt to be a liability than an asset. The meaning of the term depends, to a large extent, on the context in which it is seen. Similarly, if we are told that a person is "cool, industrious, capable, forceful, intelligent, effective," we have a very different picture from one who is "warm, industrious, capable, forceful, intelligent, and effective." The difference in the basic orientation of the organized view of the personality originates in the cool-warm difference, and it changes the meaning of all the items in the list.

An experiment following these ideas illustrates the principle, mentioned before, that behavior depends on the organized perception, not on the "real" world. Groups of classes were told they would have a new instructor and were asked to rate his performance. To "help" them, they were told a little about him—he is married; about so-and-so many years old; most of his friends think he is a rather cold person. Half the descriptions said ". . . think he is a rather warm person." The two descriptions were passed out to the classes, every other person getting a different one. The instructor had a discussion, being careful to behave midway between warm and cold. In the evaluation, half the class—those who were told he was cold—saw him as cold. Further, observers recorded the students' behavior. There was much more participation from those who were told he was warm. What they did depended on what they saw; what they saw depended on the organization set up by the key word.

In another experiment two groups of men were asked to describe the personality of a man on the basis of a picture and a brief description of what he does. One group consisted of union members of a central labor council; the other group consisted of industrial-relations and personnel men from industry. Both groups were shown the same picture and the same description, but management representatives were told it was a union officer, while the union representatives were told it was a member of management. In each case the description of the man given them was reinterpreted by them to fit their already existing view of what union men or management men were like, and the personalities described were quite different, each molded to harmonize with present organizations. Although each group had the same set of "facts" about the man to work on, they selected and altered them quite differently. It is entirely possible that members of the two groups, meeting in bargaining, could talk about such a man or about an issue in such a way that they used very nearly the same words but never really referred to the same thing.

As a last resort, we often provide the distortion in memory. A fact is retained in memory as part of an organized system there. If it does not fit well, it tends to be modified to fit into the essential character of the pattern of memory. The well-known changes that take place in a rumor as it is heard, remembered, and retold are an example of this kind of change. A graphic example can be seen in an experiment on memory for visual figures. Two groups of people were shown a series of figures and asked to reproduce them later. One of the figures looked like this: O-O . The group who were told it was a symbol for eyeglasses reproduced it later like this: OᴑO . The group who were told it was a symbol for dumbbells reproduced it like this: O=O. The same "fact" was modified in memory to fit the essential character of the memory system.

The nine-dot problem, earlier in this chapter, offers another example of this same change in memory. Ask your friends to solve it. Many of them will say, "I've seen that one, but I can't remember the answer." Even though the solution is, in a sense, striking, a great many people remember the problem and forget the solution. The well-organized "square" remains in memory. The awkward solution, violating good organization, disappears.

The fact of these psychological mechanisms which lead us to select and distort facts puts an even greater emphasis on our communications techniques. If we are to attempt to communicate in the interests of changing another's mind and action, we must be keenly aware of the fact that he will tend to distort what he hears on the basis of his emotions, that he may overlook the communication or modify it in terms of his already existing attitudes and organizations. More than ever, this fact emphasizes the need to tailor our communications, not on the basis of the content of what we have to say, but on the basis of the attitudes and motivations of the person at whom we are aiming. Also, it underlines the importance of waiting to find out from the other person some clue to what he heard, rather than assuming that he heard the same thing that we heard ourselves say. Realizing the possibilities of distortion, we are led to be doubly careful to check the degree and kind of distortion when the communicated material goes from outside of the speaker, where it is heard by him, to inside the listener, where it is interpreted by him.

Rejection of the media of communication

Still another psychological mechanism which acts to impede communication lies in the fact that people tend, in the interest of simplifying the problem of receiving information from the environment, to evaluate the whole medium of information through which information is received, and to accept or reject the medium and everything it carries, rather than to have to make specific judgments on separate items. Thus, for example, all of us have thrown advertising circulars out of the mail without giving them more than a casual glance. We have a general organization of the sources of communication, and we act on the implicit theory that there is a low probability of getting important information from this one. The medium is seen as one which carries certain sorts of material; since it isn't a kind of material which we particularly want, we reject the whole content without analysis. House organs probably often meet the same fate, and in many cases it seems impossible to make them into good communication media without changing their entire character in the minds of the potential recipients.

The extent to which this kind of rejection can go is shown in a survey conducted by the Treasury Department in connection with the war-bond drive which has been mentioned before. As part of the campaign, a pamphlet on bonds was mailed to every household in certain parts of the country. A check on the effectiveness of the pamphlet was conducted by interviewing a sample of the recipients in Baltimore. In spite of the fact that the pamphlet had been in every mailbox, two weeks later only 17 per cent of the people even recognized it when they were allowed to examine it, and 83 per cent of the people could not even remember having seen it two weeks before. Of the 17 per cent who recognized it, only one-third remembered having seen the cover, and consequently only about 10 per cent were even exposed to the material within. This gloomy result is probably characteristic of the fate of information carried in many media of communication where a generalized negative evaluation has been made of the kind of facts that are apt to be found within.

Wherever a form of communication has become routine and stereotyped, it is liable to be judged in terms of the kind of information usually contained, and hence may become almost useless for conveying any other kind. Many of the techniques of communication that are in use in industry today no doubt are characterized in such a manner, and many of them suffer by it. In addition to the aura that the house organ has, which may make it inappropriate for carrying certain messages, such media as the annual report, weekly luncheons with supervisory groups, speeches on the occasion of awarding service pins, and the like, may tend to be stereotyped by the listener. "They usually talk about such-and-such, and so there's no need to listen." Formalized and routinized methods of communication are always in need of a constant reevaluation and analysis to determine how the communication channel itself is seen by the recipients, for the effect of its content is largely determined by the listeners' perception of the medium.

All these things act as barriers to communication and must be taken into consideration in planning communication. The distortion of information under the influence of the listener's motivations, the psychological mechanisms rejecting or distorting items, and the tendency to reject whole media of information are all examples of impediments to communication which stem from the problem of the individual's organizing an ambiguous environment into a sensible pattern in which he can live comfortably and securely.

One further problem arises which makes communication difficult, in addition to the simple facts of organizations: the patterns that people make of the environment are tentative, and are retained, modified, or discarded to some extent in terms of the degree to which they seem to be successful in orienting the individual's behavior toward goals. In other words, the Law of Effect referred to in Chapter 2 acts as a continual check on tentative organizations, which function in the manner of hypotheses which are tentatively adopted until they are tested and seem to work in leading to rewards or in avoiding punishment. A preliminary acceptance, on the part of the listener, of certain items of information may often be reversed later when they are found not to agree with practice, and consequently not to be a good guide to action. The result is to make the particular item increasingly difficult to communicate later, and perhaps to make the medium through which it was originally communicated less effective in carrying other messages.

Examples of this phenomenon would be the countless situations where an announced policy speaks of "an open door, where everyone is invited to bring his problems to the president if he likes." However, it is generally known that this is not really the case, and that if anyone did go to the president, everyone involved would be bowled over with surprise. Such a policy is quickly rejected by subordinates as insincere and meaningless, and they live by the facts as they experience them, rather than by the words. Similar fates probably meet such statements as "We are all one big happy family," when in fact everyone acts as if they were not, or "We promote people here strictly on the basis of what they do," when in fact one sees promotions occurring on the basis of seniority, acquaintances, and the like. In cases of these sorts the verbal communication is rejected because it does not fit the dimensions of reality in practice, and to use the information in organizing a picture of the environment would be to violate the Law of Effect and to act on the basis of principles which would not lead to rewards.

The implications of this for the communicator seem to be that he must be very careful of the relation between his statements and the kind of events that are going to occur. If the statement is worth making and has value in its content, it is important to see that it is backed up in practice. Otherwise it may be accepted at first, found to be a liability in action, and discarded with resentment toward the communicator for misleading. If such a thing happens repeatedly, then the communicator, as a medium, may be rejected and ignored because he is stereotyped as an unreliable informant. Often it would be a better policy, from a communications point of view, to refrain from making statements which one hopes were true but which might not hold in practice, than to enjoy making the pronouncement with the subsequent risk of other statements being rejected because earlier ones failed to materialize.

In the face of a host of difficulties in communications, it seems strange that anything ever gets across. Indeed, it is difficult, and it is probably because of this difficulty that most human relationships are built in such a way that they do not demand great precision in communication except in simple specific denotations. By and large, people get along on the basis of an unexpressed realization that no two people see the world the same way, and that different people seldom mean the same thing when they speak the same words. However, in a closely interdependent organization there are many cases where the transmission of information and the changing of attitudes are essential. Some points to improve this necessary communication can be derived from an examination of the very difficulties themselves.

Techniques of communication

The material to be communicated must be tailored on the basis of the listener's view of the situation rather than the content of the information itself; this point has already been stressed. Unfortunately, most of us are so used to building statements in terms of content, and so clear about what we are trying to say, that it is difficult to accomplish this reversal in approach. However, the greatest single aid to communication would probably be learning to *tailor information on the basis of the recipient's organization* of the situation.

A good example of the failure to tailor the information to the other person is often found in the booklets describing the company that are issued in many plants. In one specific case, the company published an expensive booklet on glossy paper in full color, for the purpose of providing indoctrination and orientation for new employees. An interview study of a group of employees who had been with the company for six months or less brought out the discouraging fact that not a single one of them had read the document. Why? The pamphlet, though beautifully done, was written for management to read. It told that there were many thousands of employees of the organization; that the investment per worker was so-and-so much; that the company paid an annual wage bill in astronomical figures. Information such as this is interesting and meaningful to the men who wrote the booklet, to their immediate superiors, and to the vice-presidential board which probably had to pass on it. However, the bulk of the new employees were girls in their teens for whom these figures, and particularly this way of stating them, had no meaning or interest at all. The money that was spent on the brochure was virtually a total loss.

Another method that would probably improve communications would be to *transmit information in small units*. A large organized mass of material tends to threaten existing patterns in the listener and so may be rejected. Small units transmitted little by little carry the same message over a period of time without the same likelihood of rejection. Cumulatively they may effect the change where they would be rejected out of hand if they were presented at once.

The importance of finding out what the listener has heard has come up repeatedly. As a check on what was, in fact, communicated, it is essential for the communicator to *provide an opportunity for "feedback"* from the recipient. Unless one has some way of finding out what was heard, either by observing subsequent behavior or by some kind of restatement, communication must remain pretty much a matter of shooting in the dark, with very uncertain results.

One of the most effective ways to provide for feedback, and at the same time an effective technique for communication, is to *provide an opportunity for participation* on the part of the recipient. If the material and situation are such that the recipient can be brought into a discussion and encouraged to state problems and solutions in his own words, many of the difficulties are overcome. For one thing, a constant index of his view of the matter is present. For another, he becomes involved in the material himself, so it is less apt to be a threat to his existing organizations, and consequently it is less apt to be rejected or distorted to protect private views of the world. Finally, such a practice frees the listener from the one-sidedness of much communication where he passively listens to what he is told. Now he participates in it and is part of it, and he no longer has to reject the material on the grounds that being told threatens his egoistic need-satisfactions and feeling of independence. Eliciting participation is often a relatively costly process in time and effort, and at first glance it seems unnecessary and prohibitively expensive. However, the returns are potentially very great, and with practice it becomes much easier to accomplish.

Changing attitudes

One other point should be considered before we leave the problem of communication. We are usually interested in communication with the aim of changing other people's attitudes and with the eventual aim of changing their behavior. We want people to stop doing something they are doing or to start doing something they aren't doing, and we have the feeling that their behavior flows from their attitudes and that if their attitudes were different the behavior would change. Because of this we try to influence attitudes. Since this is so large a part of the field of communication, it is a good idea to look a little more closely at the problem of attitudes.

We often speak of someone "having" an attitude, as if the attitude were a tangible and separate thing, in much the same sense that he might have a Chevrolet rather than a Ford. This way of speaking about it has led us to try to change "his" attitude by persuasion, sweet reasonableness, or attack. Certainly all of us have been discouraged by the fact that we do not seem to change attitudes in this manner very often, and that, indeed, attack often seems to strengthen the person in the attitude he "has." If we look back over what we have said so far about the problem of an individual's making sense out of his complex environment, we see that we should not think of him as "having" an attitude but rather as having organized the world in a certain way. In this sense the word "attitude" should not be used as a noun, but rather as an adverb that modifies the verb "to see." An attitude is a way of seeing things. To attack it as "his" attitude is to miss the meaning of the organization of the other person's perception of the world. Instead, we must try to see the way in which he sees things and then help him to see other things there.

On a hot day the surf looks inviting and cool. We do not at all have the feeling that this is an attitude in us. Regardless of the past experience that leads it to look this way, within ourselves the invitingness is simply a part of the view of the surf. To try to attack this view by argument is likely to leave us quite unmoved. Indeed, if the argument continues, we may well come to a point where we defend it as a point of honor *because* it is attacked. If someone wanted to change our behavior (that is, to keep us from going swimming), it would be more appropriate for him to realize that it looks cool and inviting and to work from there. Perhaps he could point out other similarly cooling things that required less exertion, such as a long drink on a shaded porch. Perhaps he could lead us to see other things in the surf that would change our perception, such as the undertow or the danger of sunburn. His doing these things might change the way we see the surf and might consequently change our behavior. In this way he would have changed the adverbial character of the attitude, that is, he would have changed the way we saw. He would not have changed the attitude in the sense of having attacked and modified something that we had.

An attitude is not something that resides in the person. It is a characteristic of the way he sees things. This leads us to take quite different means to modify it. Usually it is better to work indirectly to do this rather than to attack it broadside. A particularly good example of this in an industrial situation appears in the chapter dealing with egoistic needs. You will remember that the foremen in a production-line plant had tended to refer to their subordinates by payroll numbers, and that it was felt that this was a poor practice. It would not be surprising if, having realized this, the training department had had a series of meetings in which they exhorted the foremen to "be human," to "remember that the other person is a human and has interests and feelings like you." This would be the direct attack on attitude viewed as something the other person "has" and something we want him to get rid of. Instead, in this case, it was realized that this failure to treat the subordinates as individuals came from a failure to see them as individuals, and the treatment was to try to change the way they were seen. The indirect approach of having the foremen gather personal history data on their subordinates was a way to change the things they saw in them, and indirectly it changed their attitudes. Usually lectures on "treating the other fellow as a real person" are singularly unsuccessful. Here the attempt to help someone *see* the other fellow as a real person was very successful. In many ways it is a model of the indirect approach to attitude change.

In another, very different case, it is possible to see the same sort of indirect approach to a modification of attitude by changing the way things are seen. A large utility was concerned with the public's attitude toward the cost of service. Survey data indicated that many people thought the cost was too high. A series of advertisements were prepared and run in which the cost was argued directly, showing how expensive it was to provide service, how little the cost had risen in relation to other rises, and the like. This is typical of the direct attack on an attitude that occurs when we think of the attitude as something the person has and as a thing which is subject to attack and change. Surveys taken after these ads showed that there was either no more favorable attitude toward cost or else an increase in suspicion about the cost, since the company felt it had to talk too much to protect itself. Another series of ads were run at about the same time, however, which did not approach this problem directly, but simply showed the case of a new employee coming to work and learning about the job and becoming part of the community through the job. Surveys taken after this ad showed a general increase in the favorable response to the company and, much to the surprise of the public-relations department, a striking increase in the favorable response to costs. Although this subject was not mentioned or implied in the message, the ad had succeeded in changing the way in which the particular aspect having to do with cost was changed.

This view of attitudes has real implications for management's perennial concern over "morale." It very often happens that, when there are difficulties, someone in the company says, "The morale around here has gone to pot. We'd better get the X Company in to do a morale survey, and then see what we can do about it." After the horrible and discouraging results of the survey, an "attack on morale" is planned. Usually it is relatively fruitless, and everyone concerned is forced, in self-defense, to think that the whole society is changing, that they don't hire the kind of people they used to when they were young, and that the attitudes in the plant are just bound to be difficult. Much of the difficulty probably lies in the view of what "morale" is. Whatever it is, it is not an identifiable possession of the individual worker. It is not a thing to be found and exorcised like the devils of the days of witchcraft. What we mean by morale is the effects of the way the plant force see their working environment. It is the result of certain ways of seeing. To deal with it we need to understand as clearly as possible how they do see it, and then to consider what things within them or within the environment lead to this kind of perception. Then, perhaps, we are ready to try to alter the process of seeing and, in this way, the morale.

SUMMARY

1. Communication is important to the superior as part of his job of directing the work of his subordinates and of creating a situation in which they can help him to get the

job done. At the same time the importance of communication to the subordinate is clear in terms of his problem of making a pattern for himself of the nature of the job and his role, and to help him keep a clear picture of the world in which he operates.

2. The chief difficulty seems to arise by virtue of the fact that people tend to organize information into meaningful wholes, and in the process they may receive different information from what the communicator intended to convey. More specifically, hopes and fears may serve to modify and distort information. There is a tendency to reject and distort items on the basis of already existing organizations of the subject, and to reject whole media of communication and to render them ineffective. Finally, it is important to keep practice in line with statements because of the role of the Law of Effect in the acceptance or rejection of communicated material.

3. In an attempt to find ways to improve communications, on the basis of these difficulties and the nature of people, we have seen the importance of tailoring material in terms of the recipient's organization of the subject. We have also seen the possibility of communicating in small units, the importance of a "feedback" which will allow the communicator to check what is actually getting across, and the value of participation as a technique for effecting communication. Both the problems and the solutions in the area of communication are part of every other phase of industrial problems. Wherever we turn in considering problems of human beings at work—in the area of leadership, of training, or wherever—we see evidences of these same barriers and the same techniques for overcoming them. In many senses, good communications seems to be the key to many of the problems in our industrial society.

4. In using communication to change attitudes, we must remember that an attitude is a way of seeing things. The

word "attitude" is not a noun; it is an adverb modifying the
verb "to see." Indirect approaches to changing the way
people see things are much more apt to produce the change
in behavior than are attempts to change an attitude by force
of argument.

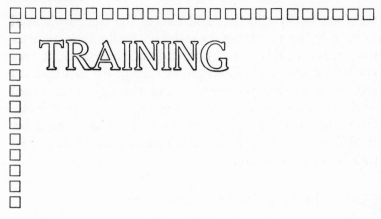

CHAPTER 5

TRAINING

Whenever we think about the problem of utilizing the human resources of an industrial organization, we almost inevitably turn to a consideration of the problem of training. Probably no other staff function has become so much elaborated, so firmly established, and so widespread as the training department. Much of this growth has been due to a recognition of the extreme importance of modifying the behavior of members of the organization. For instance, in one of the large aircraft plants during the war, the company was asked by a manpower commission to make a list of the priority of members of management. The person who could least be spared was the top manager; the next most indispensable man on the list was the head of the training department. This was an unusual situation, but it reflected a realization of the importance to the company of being able to take in large groups of people and quickly make them maximally effective, and also of the company's need to be able, by retraining, to maintain flexibility in production. Although this is a rare ranking of importance, it may not have been far off. However, in spite of the fact that the problem is extremely important, and although a great deal of time and money and effort has been poured into training, the result has not always been as successful as it might be. It will pay us to examine the mechanisms of industrial training in some detail.

The superior shapes (trains) his work force

We have looked at the nature of leadership in Chapter 3 and have seen some of the training functions of the leader there. The superior's job is to get help from his subordinates. He has subordinates because he is responsible for more work than he can do himself. He is successful only if, and to the extent that, he is able to enlist their cooperation and to direct their efforts toward the productive aims of the organization. In the process of directing their efforts and teaching them what needs to be done, he is bound to be a trainer. A large part of the difference between an old and new employee, or between a good and bad employee, is apt to be in the way in which he does his job. The superior's objective, then, is to train him in the kinds of attitudes and the kinds of skills that will insure production. In the early stages of association it is almost impossible for the subordinate to have any sort of interaction with the superior without some sort of training taking place. The subordinate learns certain kinds of things about the job and the plant and the superior. This kind of training always takes place in on-the-job interaction, and it is inevitable that the superior will be a trainer. The only question is whether he will do it consciously and properly, or without paying attention to it and haphazardly. We also saw that the superior must help the subordinate to achieve a new and stable organization of the work place and of the job. He must help him to make sense of his part of the world, and the particular sense he makes of it will have a great deal to do with his attitudes, with his morale, and with his productivity. He must be helped to learn what is expected of him, what his resources are, what the rules and values of the organization are, and the like. He must be helped to achieve a coherent organization of the environment which will include himself, his job, his superior, and his future goals. In doing all these things the leader is inevitably a trainer.

In still another sense, the superior is inevitably a trainer. As we look back to Chapter 2, we see, in considering the problem of dependence at work, that the superior controls most of the values in the work situation and, through his administration of these values, is constantly supplying rewards and punishments to his subordinates. Further, in considering the Law of Effect, we saw that the behavior of the subordinates tends to be modified in the direction of repeating behavior which seems to lead to reward and eliminating those behavior patterns which seem not to. Because of this, and because of the dependence of the subordinate on the superior, the leader *is* training all day and every day. He is, whether he likes it or not, continually using the Law of Effect and shaping behavior by the administration of rewards and punishments, and consequently it behooves him to be aware of it and do it carefully. The leader cannot escape his role as a trainer, and although he often tends to ignore it, he continues to function as one. Consequently it is important to be aware of the function as explicitly as possible, so that he may use his training function to shape behavior toward the proper ends, rather than at random.

In many cases we try to escape this responsibility and hope that we can undo an existing bad situation by devoting a weekly half hour to a statement of what would be a better one, rather than to work within the bad situation to correct it. The many cases of foreman training in industry offer a good example of this. Members of management at some level are dissatisfied with the kind of supervision exercised by the foremen. Consequently they direct the training department to teach the foremen how to be leaders. Essentially they are saying, "You tell the men what kinds of behavior is desired, that is, what kind of behavior will lead to reward on the job. I don't care to or haven't the time to be careful myself to be sure that the kinds of behavior desired actually do lead to reward for them and that other behaviors do not." Unfortunately, the human organism is not built that way. No matter what we tell them is the desired behavior, no matter what we say is the path to reward, behavior will be shaped by what is seen by the individual to lead to reward and punishment in the actual situation. It is impossible for the superior to shrug off the training function.

The things that the superior does to exercise his role as a trainer are many and varied. The way he says "hello" often indicates approval or disapproval. He may not mean it to, but the subordinate's interpretation is the thing that counts. If a curt "good morning" is felt as a punishment, it functions as such whether it is a sign of a job poorly done or is merely a result of the superior's hangover. All the little things—the manner in which a suggestion is received, the kind of responsibility given a subordinate, the word of praise or correction, all the content of the interaction between superior and subordinate—go to make up the rewards and punishments that shape behavior.

This does not mean that it is only in the little social interactions on the job that the training occurs. It occurs in the kinds of things that the foreman picks out for praise or blame. These become important dimensions in the employee's mind. Are they really important, or are they just easy ones to talk about? When the superior says, "Why don't you ever sweep up the shavings around your lathe?" does he really mean to emphasize housekeeping, or is it just that he can't quite put in words the fact that the lathe operator is upsetting the group by his attitude? He needs to be clear which behavior needs changing and what the effect of his statement will be. When he describes the job to a new employee, which things does he pick to tell him about? Are these the important dimensions? Certainly they will tend to stand out until the subordinate learns more about it. Here, too, is a place for decision. When he describes the reasons for a promotion, a transfer, or a layoff, he is underlining certain aspects of the job. When he reports higher management's views, when he says, "Oh, are you still doing that? Don't bother about that . . ."—in all these cases he is shaping the subordinate's view of the job and taking part in the training process.

These are the things that do the training, no matter what is said in the training classroom. These are the things that the superior cannot avoid. Since he is necessarily in the business of administering reward and punishment and shaping behavior by the Law of Effect, it becomes particularly important for him to be aware of it and to pattern his own behavior as carefully as possible, rather than to let it happen without plan. For, as surely as he trains his subordinates with his own actions, he will have to live with and be responsible for the kind of behavior he has built into them. His success depends on what they do, and this is his chance to make that behavior be what he wants it to be.

The industrial culture

Still another factor tends to make it important for the line superior to administer training, rather than to try to palm it off on a formal classroom session. We discussed briefly in Chapter 2 the problem of the individual in making sense out of an ambiguous environment, and in coming to a stable organization of his world in terms of which he can live. Among a group of people as within a plant or within a department, such organizations become a recognizable culture. It has considerable value to the members of the group, to direct their behavior, and it develops a good deal of resistance to change. When the behavior which must be modified is within such a culture, it is particularly important that the change arise within it and that it be supported by the values of the culture. The attempt to impose change by a real outsider is typically unsuccessful, and the formal training department is usually, because of its staff role, outside the control of the values of the culture.

The individual in an organization is imbedded in a world in which he sees, in addition to people and things, all sorts of barriers and threats, goals, and paths to goals. These are the things which the person must organize for himself, and in terms of which his behavior must be directed. In a group of human beings which continues through time, there develops a common fund of experience and a certain amount of communality in their experience. Out of this develop "proper" ways of behaving—ways of working and loafing, ways of cooperating or resisting, attitudes toward the work and toward authority, and the like. These patterns are not explicit and formal, but they are potent. Their structure and organization provide a stable and secure framework in which to operate.

The laws of such a culture or spirit of an organization are easy for an outsider to sense, although they are often very difficult for a newcomer to learn. Some organizations have an aura of suspicion, tension, and fear that strike one immediately, while some are freer and more relaxed. In some cases it is proper to do one's assignment as quickly and well as possible and ask for or be ready for more; in some cases it is proper to stretch out a job until another one is given. Sometimes it is proper to look forward to the coffee hour and make it last, and in others the main focus is on the work, with relief something that one takes if it can be worked in. In some groups it is proper to take an assignment grudgingly and do it and no more, while in others it is proper to meet the superior more than halfway in cooperation and to try to anticipate what he wants. All these things and many more are dimensions of the culture of the organization, and they have great power and value. Violations of their principles by members of the group are often immediately and harshly punished by social pressures of ostracism and ridicule, and little real comfort can be found until one senses the rules of the culture and learns to live by them.

Consider the situation when a new typist comes to work in the office. At 10:30 one of the girls asks her to join them for coffee, and she says she's finishing a report so she can't go. The old hand turns to her companions and says, "Get her. Only here two hours and she's already bucking to be boss!" The newcomer will quickly learn the office culture. Although she probably cannot stop the report at this stage in the relationship and join the coffee group, it is a likely bet that the next morning she will be ready to go when the others are. She has learned something about the importance of finishing your job in this office. She is going to have to work with these girls and derive many of her satisfactions from interaction with them. Further, she is protected by the fact that if they take this attitude she will not lose out on promotions by taking it, too. She can hardly afford to do anything else. She is learning the culture, and the culture is determining the way she will work. It is taking over part of the leader's function.

The existence of such firm patterns of behavior is of great help to an individual in making it possible for him to form a stable organization of his environment, and therefore the patterns acquire considerable power and value of their own. Because they do provide this kind of help, and because their continued existence offers security, they acquire a resistance to change which can be a potent barrier to the superior who wants to modify behavior.

Many of the aspects of such a cultural pattern must be changed by superiors in the course of modifying behavior and directing the efforts of their subordinates. It is often very difficult for the leader to make such changes when they conflict with well-established patterns policed by the group. The leader, however, has real leverage in that he is, in a sense, within the value system of the group, and that he controls many of the rewards and paths to goals that are involved. In a moment we will look in a little detail at the things the leader can do to make such changes, and the ways in which the group itself can be utilized to make change, but first let us examine the problem of the outside staff agency in changing the culture of a group.

Encapsulated training

When the training department is directed to make a change, it has a very special problem. Let us consider the problem of foreman training referred to above. The foremen come to class to be told how to be foremen. On the job they have a particular role and style that is recognized by their subordinates. They are seen in a particular way by their superiors. They have a set of techniques for dealing with people which are the basis of their present success. It is by behaving this way that they have gotten where they are. The training supervisor now tells them to do things differently. What are they to do? If they go back on the job to behave differently, they are insecure for several reasons. First, they have just given up their accustomed ways and are about to try techniques which they are not sure they can do and which they may understand imperfectly anyway. Secondly, not only does the foreman no longer have the same role in his own eyes, but he has a new role in his subordinates' eyes. The change makes them insecure and uneasy and difficult to deal with, and adds problems to those contributed by the newness of his own techniques. Finally, he is fearful of his new role in his superior's eyes. They have seen him relatively successful in his old ways of operating (or he wouldn't be foreman), and now he must change. Won't they say "Old Joe is slipping"? Nowhere—in his own eyes, in the view of his subordinates, or in that of his superiors—is there any security in the new forms of behavior. Only the training department stands behind him. How much safer for him to do exactly what he has been doing all along and what has brought him at least some success so far!

However, the training department also has a culture and controls a set of values. For the foreman it is a continuation of much of the pattern that he was used to in school. Here is the series of rows of chairs with a figure who stands in front and speaks authoritatively, and who passes out approval and disapproval for certain kinds of behavior. He must attend these meetings, and within the meetings he will fit into the cultural patterns of this group as surely and as quickly as possible. We have really put him into a new situation in which he must learn something. In the first place he has a job, and he has learned a good deal about how to behave there. Now he must go to meetings. The company clearly wants him to go. The trainer has certain values and standards. He must learn to behave in this pattern. The usual result is that as the meetings progress the foreman progresses in that from meeting to meeting he behaves more and more the way the trainer wants him to— within the meeting. He learns to say the kinds of things the trainer approves of and to work in terms of the trainer's frame of reference—within the classroom. However, when he leaves the meeting and goes back to the job he tends to do exactly as he did before. There is little reason to change. On the job he gets reward and approval from one group of people for doing certain kinds of things; within the classroom he gets reward and approval from another group of people for doing rather different things. There is no real reason to carry over from one to the other. Fortunately, the two are usually well separated in time and space, so that they don't come in contact. Indeed, the foreman would be taking a ridiculous risk to follow the trainer's suggestions unless there were clear and consistent evidence at every point *outside the classroom* that his superior's values coincide exactly with the trainer's. This very seldom occurs. It is almost impossible, if the line superior feels that he is not responsible for training and that it should be turned over to the staff department. In the absence of this unity the foreman must do one thing in one situation and another in the second. On the job he follows the culture of the work group and the line superior, and in the classroom he follows the values of the classroom group and the training supervisor. The training is encapsulated within the classroom; the progress he makes from week to week stays there. He tends to leave it there rather than to take the risk of trying it out outside. The smart student will be careful not to accept change in one group and meet an unchanged superior on the job.

It is not only on the job that we allow this encapsulation of training to grow up. It is quite as customary to say to a new graduate on the job, "That may be the way you learned to do it in college, but you're on the job now, so just forget that. We'll show you how it's really done." Here we have let the split between the trainer and the supervisor grow as wide as possible. In many ways it is necessary, for the training organization involved in our educational system is too large and too specialized to be done as part of an apprentice program. However, here too, it probably would be of benefit both to the schools and to the employers if there were a closer harmony between the two in terms of the kinds of values and skills and attitudes that were taught, so that it would minimize the gulf between them. Then it might be more nearly possible for us to train students to take a job, instead of merely training them and having them take a job afterward.

The line superior must train

Because of these problems the line superior must do the training. Not only do we find that he is doing the training all day and every day, but he is the appropriate person to do it. Because he controls so many of the values within the group, because he is a part of the culture of the group, and because of the isolation of the staff man from the culture and authority of the group, the responsibility falls on the line superior. Since he is the one who possesses these characteristics, he is the person in a position to do the training. Because of the meaning of his role as a leader, it is his proper function. He must continually shape the behavior of his subordinates to create a situation in which they can help him to get the job done. He must create the conditions under which they can achieve a stable organization of their environment on the job which will lead them to produce the kind of behavior that is directed toward the aims of their group and the larger organization of which it is a part. All these things combine to thrust the training role on the line superior, and there is little he can do to avoid it.

What happens in a typical training situation? Let us go back to the foreman-training problem. Management has felt some lacks in the first line of supervision and has directed the training department to put on a good course for the foremen. The foremen have a series of lectures, with perhaps demonstrations and role-playing thrown in, and they learn a series of precepts to guide their action on the plant floor. They may even be given a card to carry in their pockets with the rules on it, so that they won't forget: don't take credit for a subordinate's ideas; don't bawl a man out in front of his fellow workers; delegate responsibility to subordinates; let a man feel that he has as big a job as he can handle; etc. The foreman's superiors now hope that he will go forth and sin no more. But will these slogans be as effective in training the foreman as the administration of them in practice by his own superiors? Have the superiors carefully policed the transmission of suggestions and new ideas to see that the credit is going to the originator? Do they reward the foreman for creating the condition where his subordinate had an idea and forwarded it and for not taking the credit, or do they in effect punish him by rewarding only the man with the new idea? Has the foreman had a clear and consistent example of *his* superiors giving him credit for his own ideas? It seems highly likely that the foreman will be much more apt to modify his behavior to fit the precept if it is reinforced by appropriate rewards and punishments relevant to the behavior itself, rather than simply announced by the training supervisor as a "good thing." If the foreman's superior does not see that behavior tailored to the precept is followed by reward, the foreman cannot afford to live by it. He had much better either forget it quickly or take it to another shop where he will fare better with it.

The superior is quite apt to feel that he is too busy with other things to school himself to pay attention to all the little details that are involved in such a regimen of approval and disapproval. He has, he says, to see to the production;

he can't spend all his time worrying about how his subordinates feel about things. Such a point of view seems to be compounded equally of a failure to see his objectives clearly, of a reluctance to see his own role in relation to his subordinates, and of an attempt to escape from the difficult job of dealing with his subordinates as people. If he sees that his objective is to accomplish production through his subordinates, if he sees that he must create a situation where they can help him and must shape their behavior in the desired directions, then he cannot escape the responsibility of dealing with them in such a way as to train them. He must question what things he can do to help them to acquire an organization of the environment which will elicit the desired behavior.

As soon as we begin to see the role of the line superior in training, it becomes apparent that the man to do the training is the trainee's own superior. *His* superior trains *him*, and so on. The end result is that the only man to initiate the training is the president himself. At first glance this seems a forbidding and ridiculous conclusion, but it is inescapable. Wherever the matter of the training is an over-all policy or a company-wide problem, the training must start at the top and work down. Without it we are little better off to start in the middle. Wherever the change is introduced we run the risk of the changed individual running up against his unchanged superior, and necessarily either forfeiting the approval of his superior or giving up his newly taught practices. A change can be introduced at whatever point it can be said with certainty that every step in the organizational hierarchy above that point is in complete agreement in theory and practice with the content of the training. In the case of broad strategic matters, such as problems of leadership and interpersonal relations within the organization, this point is usually only at the very top of the company. When the content of the training is relatively circumscribed—such as training in shop safety practices or teaching a new clerk how to write a sales ticket—it can probably safely be done at the level of the person who has immediate responsibility for the operation in question. However, to avoid the possibility of a change through training being in conflict with the rewards and punishments of an unchanged superior, the only safe rule is to demand certainty of agreement on the policy at every step above the level at which the change is to be introduced.

At first glance, this approach seems to cut the heart out of the job of the training department in an industrial organization. On the contrary, however, it leaves a considerable function for the staff in training and, moreover, restores them to responsibility for jobs which they have the authority to accomplish, rather than asking them to compete with the power of their students' superiors. The training supervisor can now play the proper staff role. He can consult with and help and advise the appropriate line officer. He can collect facts and make suggestions relative to the existence of training needs. He can supply his expert assistance to the line man in the form of a plan for techniques for training, times and amounts, the need for refresher and continuation, and the like. He can consult with the line man on the way in which the proposed training program is likely to modify behavior and the implications of this change for the objectives of the organization. He can work with the line superior on the way in which the training program will be tied to the superior's own on-the-job reinforcement of the policies. However, the line man will do most of the training. In some cases it may even be that the staff man is the best man to conduct certain training sessions—using his ability to start discussions, and the like—but only with the fullest kind of coordination with the line superior regarding on-the-job follow-up, and probably ideally only with the line man's presence and actual backing.

The role of the staff training expert—
augmentation and reduction

This view of the staff man's relation to training makes
sense of the difference between the staff and the line. The
staff function is one of support and advice. Ideally, the relation might work something like this in practice: Either the
line man senses a need for training in his group, or the staff
man points out to him available information which suggests
that training is needed. In either case, the decision rests
with the line man. The line man now asks what should be
done. The staff man can suggest ways which have been used
and which might be applicable. The line man sets the objectives of the training, with the counsel of his staff helper.
In the light of these objectives the staff helps the line plan
a session (or a series of sessions). The line man conducts
the sessions and goes again to the staff man to tell him how
it went and to get suggestions about how to do it differently,
or how to go on. Throughout this process, the key decisions
are all made by the line, and the training is all handled with
the force of the line behind it. This is the proper relation
between the two even if the line man is a first-level foreman
and the staff man the $15,000-a-year head of the personnel
department. The force of the decision to train, the method,
and the authority behind the training must come from the
line. The staff is without authority here. Its only influence
comes from the extent to which it can help the line to see
a particular course of action as justified.

This does not leave the staff in a powerless position. Indeed, this very lack of authority which seems to be a weak-
ness in the staff man's position is actually a great source of
strength, because it protects him from slipping into some
very common failings in the use of authority. Let us examine this in a little more detail. Going back to Chapter 2, we
said that all the behavior of an individual is directed toward

an attempt to satisfy needs, and that any particular behavior is the result of forces arising from these motivational
problems. Any change in his behavior, consequently, will
come from either an attempt to increase the satisfaction of
needs or an attempt to avoid a decrease in the possibilities
of need-satisfaction. We should be clear at this point, as we
were in discussing the Law of Effect, that we are talking
about what the individual *sees* as being likely to increase
or decrease his possibilities for need-satisfaction. Regardless
of what we, outside, know to be true, his behavior will follow his organization of the environment. Further, if Mr. A
wants B to change his behavior, A must use one of these
two mechanisms: he must lead B to see either that this
particular behavior will augment his (B's) possibilities of
need-satisfaction, or else that not producing this particular
behavior will lead to a reduction of B's possibilities of need-
satisfactions. Mr. A may or may not appear in the picture as directly responsible for either the augmentation or the reduction, but all his approaches—whether suggestions or threat
or promise—boil down to these possibilities.

If Mr. A is to use one of these methods—that is, of trying
to induce a change in B's behavior by promising an augmentation of the possibilities of need-satisfaction or by threatening a reduction in the possibilities—he (Mr. A) must appear
in B's eyes to control the means for need-satisfaction in the
situation. Let us look at the kind of means for need-satisfaction that the staff man and the line man respectively control.
The line authority presumably includes the right to hire and
fire, the right to promote, and, within limits, the right to assign work. In this area the line manager is well equipped
with the control of means essential to produce a change in
behavior in his subordinates. He has the wherewithal to do
the training job. On the other hand, the staff expert has in
his control only those things that arise from his qualifica-
tions as an expert—a knowledge of the situation and of pos-

sible remedies for it. These are ineffective in producing a behavior change in trainees, but he can use them to advantage in making it possible for the line manager to do a better supervisory job with his own subordinates. The staff manager can make his own expertness a tool to help the line manager to fulfill the role of the leader in the superior-subordinate relationship.

The very fact that the staff man does not have a great deal of control of the means for accomplishing need-satisfaction means that he is protected from what seems to be a common human tendency—the tendency to rely on reduction, and to equate authority with a technique of getting things done by saying, essentially, "Do it or else." In almost all cases of behavior change we have these two alternatives —either to see the change as leading to something desirable or to see it as something that must be done to avoid something undesirable. The use of augmentative techniques requires more planning and ingenuity, and it is perhaps partly for this reason that there seems to be a widespread tendency to resort to reductive methods when one has a large share of the control of the situation. In addition, there is probably a certain amount of egoistic need-satisfaction for the orderer who can say "Do it or else," and it is perhaps for this reason that, as the situation becomes complex and difficult (and the superior more insecure), the orderer tends to be even more firmly wedded to reduction as a method and even less able to see the possibilities of augmentation in the situation. Almost all the staff man can do, on the other hand, is to offer his advice and knowledge as a way for the line manager to do a better job and hence to find more need-satisfactions for himself. The staff man is protected by the structure of the organization from much of the tendency to use reduction. It is only when he begins to issue training directives himself, when he takes over the hiring responsibility, or when he "gets the ear of the boss" to an undue extent, that he develops the kind of control of the means to need-satisfaction which would allow him to be successful in reductive authority. When this happens the organization has lost the meaning of the distinction between staff and line, and the staff man's protection against an exaggerated use of reduction is gone.

The fact that the staff man does not have the means to use reductive authority is viewed as an asset because there are so many expensive by-products of this kind of leadership. It is perfectly clear that we can induce behavior changes by threatening dire consequences, if we have the power to enforce the threat. The villain of old-fashioned melodrama who tied the heroine to a log approaching a saw and said, "Now, me proud beauty, marry me or else" is a classic caricature. The black snake whip engenders a certain amount of cooperation, but it elicits a parallel measure of resentment and it does not yield much in the way of initiative. If we are, indeed, to make the subordinate's dependence as easy for him to carry as possible, and if we are to encourage active independence in him, we must look constantly for augmentative techniques rather than reductive methods in the use of authority. This is a keystone of the staff expert's role. It should equally be an important aspect of the superior's outlook as he realizes that he *is* training all day every day. In his on-the-job contacts he will have many opportunities to offer his subordinates augmentation of their possibilities for need-satisfactions, and these will be his most valuable device in shaping their behavior.

Security and seniority put increased pressure on training

Several factors which are currently growing in importance combine to put an additional emphasis on the training function. For one thing, increased job security, as it comes from contractual relations or from a tight labor market, means that any given subordinate is more likely to remain than formerly. It means that we are going to have to make what we want out of our subordinates rather than pick what we want. The fact that they are going to be with us means that it behooves us to pay special attention to the training function, so that they will help us to get the job done. In addition to this, we have seen in Chapter 2 that increased job security means an increased security in the future satisfaction of basic physical needs, and this, remembering the hierarchical character of needs, means that the higher-order —social and egoistic—needs will come into play more strongly. On the job this means that the superior's reliance must be placed less on the traditional and obvious rewards of pay and promotion, and more on the provision of rewards in the form of need-satisfactions that are in line with these higher-order needs. The superior must become more than ever alert to his opportunities to understand these motives in his subordinates and to utilize them in his daily training program.

Along with this increased security goes an increase in seniority. To say that a man stays longer on the job is another way of saying that he has more seniority. There is a current tendency to promote more on the basis of seniority than of merit, for a variety of reasons, and this means that the superior must again be particularly alert for the training implications of this policy on his work force. To promote for seniority is to reward a kind of behavior that is valuable to the company and is a social asset at the same time. However, it does not single out meritorious performance, and it takes away an opportunity to use the conventional reward and punishment implied in promotions to help shape behavior other than long service. Since this is true, the immediate superior must find other ways to modify the behavior of his subordinates, so as to direct their efforts. In place of promotions that go on the basis of seniority he must substitute augmentations of need-satisfactions in other areas. Here too, it is particularly appropriate for him to become more alert to the possibilities in the area of social and egoistic motives.

It should be pointed out here that to the extent that there is a substantial commitment to promotion from within, management must accept a large responsibility for training the men to fill the jobs they will inherit. While there is an increasing awareness of the need for executive-development programs currently, there are still many cases in which the training implications of a system of promotion by seniority are not clearly seen. Often the promotion-from-within policy seems to top management to be primarily a kind and protective gesture to the organization and its members, and one from which they should reap benefits without further ado. However, there is a real obligation to prepare the senior in advance for his promotion, both for the sake of the company and to avoid putting him into a situation where he cannot perform. To the extent that this training is adequately done, it helps to avoid the problem of promoting on the basis of seniority *in the absence of* merit. The adequately trained senior is at least ready to make the move to which his seniority entitles him.

Other factors also point in the same direction. The deskilling of jobs that has gone along with technological progress has deprived men of some of their feeling of involvement in their jobs. To maintain their motivation the superior must find other things that will provide them with satisfactions. This same deprivation has taken away some of the training that was in the job itself. When a workman did a whole job and set his own standards, his attention to his achievement did some of the training. In a more routinized setting and with compartmentalized work the job itself loses some of its meaning as a kind of built-in training. Again, the superior must make good the deficit. As we saw in Chapter 1, this kind of change in the nature of jobs has meant a great deal more interdependence on the job, as each man does part of a job and passes it on to his neighbor. This heightened interdependence means that a premium is put on the smooth working of the whole group together. Here too, the superior is responsible for the successful interaction of his group of subordinates. All these things—indeed, almost all the implications of modern industrial development—seem to conspire to put more weight on the superior's job as a trainer. He must be more explicitly aware of his training role, and he must draw more heavily on the help of the staff expert. He can no longer, if he ever could, say, "My job is production; I haven't time to worry about people." His first attention is to the effectiveness of his people in accomplishing production. Assuring this effectiveness *is* training.

Selection and training

In the face of these increasing personnel difficulties, there is a growing tendency to look to selection as a way to improve the quality of a work group. Actually, of course, selection is never a substitute for training or leadership. Ideally, all of them should contribute to the improvement. However, selection, and particularly the use of aptitude tests for the selection of personnel, has some seductive aspects that make it seem to be a general panacea for all production problems. The leader's job in shaping his work force is a difficult one. It requires constant attention to his subordinates as people, it demands that he try to see the world as they see it, and that he think long and carefully about their motives, and in the nature of the case, it is often discouragingly unsuccessful. Since this is so, it is no wonder that there is a tendency to turn to a technique which seems to promise to substitute for the difficult personnel decisions and actions the impersonal and distant cleanliness of a battery of tests that will tell us whether a man is good or not. In the face of leadership problems it is all too easy to think, "If I only had better people to start with, the problem wouldn't be so bad." Selection tests and interviews will never solve a general personnel problem. Indeed, in many cases they won't even help it very much. It is perhaps instructive to look in a little detail at the kind of help it can give.

Selection tests work on the theory that a selected population will do a better job than an unselected one. Fortunately, it has recently become possible to state accurately how much better such a selected population *can* be. The improvement we can hope for depends on three things. All other things being equal, the improvement that comes from a selected population depends on (1) the goodness (validity) of the test battery, (2) the number of people whom we can afford to reject after testing, and (3) the range of performance in our unselected work group. The first factor (validity) is a measure of the degree to which the test battery predicts accurately who will perform well. Since performance on the job is made up of a number of factors, our prediction of this performance is never perfect, and it is possible to state the general limits within which we have been able to do it in the past. The second factor (how many people we can afford to reject) states essentially the degree to which we can use the tests. In a very tight labor market we have to hire everyone who applies in order to keep the place staffed at all. Obviously in this situation there is very little point in testing if we are going to hire anyway; the tests will not improve production. As the labor market loosens, we may be able, say, to test a hundred people and hire only sixty; we reject 40 per cent. This means that the tests can be effective. Obviously, if we could reject all but the best 5 or 10 per cent on the tests, we would have a better group. However, the labor supply is hardly ever big enough to make this kind of cutoff possible. The third factor measures the spread of goodness of performance in the unselected population. If everyone on the job is as good as anyone else, and the test predicts that uniform performance, it is clear that adding more people of the same sort will not improve the group level. Since they all do the same, the new group will also do the same. If the difference between the best man on the job and the worst is 10 to 1, it is clear that if we could get everyone to be like the best man, and eliminate all those like the worst, the average of the group would go up considerably. However, we seldom have this kind of difference between the best and the worst on our jobs. In a routine production job like an automobile line, the ratio of the best to worst is more apt to be of the order of 11 to 10. In more flexible production jobs it sometimes approaches 3 to 2. Seldom does it go beyond this. If it does, we run into the tendency to simplify the job so that the cost of turnover and the difficulty of finding a replacement will be minimized. By and large the ratio of best to worst on a job will be minimized by the nature of the work process.

In these circumstances, taking the three factors that limit the improvement to be made by selection tests or interviews, at the kinds of values at which they usually operate, we can see the typical limits of possible improvement. If the number of applicants is so large that we can afford to reject 40 per cent, if the tests are as good as the best we usually find (validity, say, .45), and if the difference between the best man on the job and the worst before selection is on the order of 3 to 2, the improvement brought about by hiring only a selected group will be 4 per cent. That is, the new group, chosen entirely on the basis of our selection tests, will be only 4 per cent better than our original group, which was unselected as far as these tests are concerned. When we see these figures we realize that this is no place to rest our sole hope for improvement. It is seldom that we actually figure what improvement we hope to achieve. When we do, and when we compute it carefully, it is clear that selection (by interviews and tests) alone is not the answer. With tests of this sort and a ratio of best to worst of this sort, we should have to turn away ninety applicants for every ten hired to get even a 9 per cent improvement on the job.

It should be clear that whatever is said here applies not only to psychological tests as screening devices, but also to all the things that are used at present—to interviews, work history, school performance, letters of recommendation, and the like. Any or all of the selection methods depend on validity, cutoff, and spread in performance. Because we seldom or never conduct proper studies of the validity of interviews, and because most of us feel we can "size a man up," there is often a strong feeling that the interview is doing pretty well. It, too, is limited, under the conditions mentioned, to the same kind of 4 per cent or so improvement. Indeed, the validity of most interviews is so low that the contribution they make is considerably less than the 4 per cent we spoke of. Because we never examine them carefully, we never know what they're doing, and we rely on the "feeling" that we understand people by interviewing them.

It is hard to give comparable figures for the effects of training. There are not enough studies of the effects of training on the job to let us make a firm statement, and the mathematical limits are not statable in this case as they are in the case of selection. However, it does not seem out of the question to hope for 30 or 40 or even 50 per cent improvement from consistent training and good leadership. Indeed, some studies indicate that improvement on the job continues over a number of years, and if this is so it may well be possible to hope for improvement on the order of more than 100 per cent over initial levels with long-term good leadership and training. These figures do not indicate that training and leadership should take the place of selection, but they do suggest something of the relative importance that they should have in one's thinking about the factors that will lead to improvement on the job. However, it does not seem at all out of line to hope for something on the order of eight or ten times as much improvement from leadership and training as from selection. The selection is important; the effects of training will be limited by the kind of selection job that is initially done. We should try to do both. We should try to start out with the best group possible. Particularly where the training is long and expensive, or where the job requirements are unusual, the selection of the best applicants will be important. However, we must avoid thinking, "If I only had better people to start with, everything would be all right." This is a feeling that arises from the frustration and difficulty of dealing with people. It is a tempting delusion, but it is a delusion. Proper selection will strengthen our leadership and training, but it will not substitute for them.

The tests for the selection of executives probably fare a little better. In general, the validity of selection devices for the identification of high-level talent is much lower. However, the ratio of best to worst in managers is very much higher than, say, in lathe operators. It isn't unusual for a splendid manager to be ten times as good as a poor one. At the same time, the cutoff is likely to be higher. We need fewer executives as the organizational pyramid narrows at the top. We have a large group to draw from—particularly if we're willing to consider hiring executives away from other firms. The cutoff may well be at 1 per cent or less. In these circumstances, even with very low validities, the leverage of selection devices is increased. An improvement in performance on the order of 10 or 15 per cent is not out of the question. In the case of managers, however, a special problem arises. The limiting factor seems to be how well the situation allows them to manage. If we had better organization and leadership, managers might manage better. Under the present practices in utilizing managers, if we had perfect devices for identifying managerial talent, it probably wouldn't make an appreciable difference.

Most jobs in companies are not so difficult that we need to select an unusual person to do them. Most people, with normal skills and intelligence and a little experience, can do most jobs. We will solve a lot of our problems, not by finding better people, but by doing a better job of using the ones we have. Many companies, in recruiting at colleges, demand the top 10 or 15 per cent of the class, and assign people to jobs that anyone in the class could do. There is a complaint about the shortage of engineers while many engineers are put to dial reading, supervision of routine drawings, and the like. In America we have been traditionally profligate in our use of high-level talent. We demand the top 10 per cent as if it were in infinite supply, and we get as much as we do, often, because we hire good people and use them poorly. We have treated the top group in much the way we once did the buffalo and the forest—as if it were an inexhaustible supply. One of the clearest characteristics of the people in the top 10 per cent of the population is that there are only 10 per cent of them. As technological complexity makes more and more demands, we need more and more. As in the case of the buffalo and the forest, we suddenly reach the end. We'll solve the problem, not by better identification of high-level talent, but by better utilization of a broader mix of talent. The supply is adequate with optimal utilization; it is not necessarily adequate with less than adequate leadership.

We badly need bolder and more creative steps in the utilization of people. We need progressive risk taking in personnel policies and development practices. We need—and can afford—much higher levels of aspiration in what we can do in producing good workers and good managers.

In 1859 Lincoln said, speaking about Illinois farmland that was producing about 20 bushels of corn to the acre, "The soil has never been pushed to one-half its capacity. We need deeper plowing, analysis of soils, experiments with manures, varieties of seeds, the observance of seasons." No doubt the audience accepted the phrase "one-half its capacity" as an exaggeration permissible to campaigning politicians. They realized things could be done better—but twice as well? Hardly. Today, if an Illinois farmer can't get four times the yield, he can't afford to own the land. Similarly, in our industrial utilization of human resources, our goals should be improvements of 400 or 500 per cent. Without them we may not be able to afford to hold the land.

How do we train?

It is perhaps well, at this point, to go back over a number of factors and ask the question, "How do we train?" We have already spoken of the fact that the training job is the line manager's job, with the help, advice, and support of his staff experts. We have spoken of the fact that the superior's job is to get help from his subordinates and to direct their behavior toward the productive goals of the organization. With these things in mind, let us list a few cardinal points in the training process. They will not be exhaustive or detailed. The techniques of training have become so many and so specialized that it would be impossible to list them here. However, a series of central points can be set down.

1. There seems to be no substitute for a first step in the process: the leader must conceive, as clearly as possible, his objectives with respect to his subordinates. Just exactly what is it that he would like to have changed? There is little room for vague generalities here. The leader must ask himself searchingly and examine the work situation carefully for the areas and the items where change is needed, and he must

conceive as explicitly as possible the kind of situation he is aiming at after the change. At this stage he should probably not worry about how he is going to accomplish it but only about what he wants it to be. He can perhaps use some help from the staff expert here, but primarily it is his analysis and decision that are necessary. After all, it is his group of subordinates, and their production is his responsibility. After he has seen the objectives as clearly as possible in his own terms, he should stop to try to conceive of them in terms of the trainees. How will the changed situation look to them? Will it change their view of themselves? Their view of their jobs? Will it tend to change the existing culture of the plant or the work group? Will it alter the motivational patterns that are existing now? This step of seeing the change in the other's eyes will be most useful in gauging the possibilities of making the change, and also, later, in planning how to accomplish it.

2. The second step would probably be to review the action of the Law of Effect. To what extent is it true that the behaviors which the leader has conceived of as necessary and ideal are now followed by reward? To what extent do other, contradictory behaviors lead to reward? What can be done to eliminate this problem, to provide reward for those behaviors he wants repeated and to eliminate rewards for those behaviors he wants to be rid of? To what extent do policies and practices support the goals that he has conceived? If he wants initiative and suggestions for improving the work force, is it general practice as well as policy to reward and encourage this kind of behavior on the part of subordinates? To what extent are the policies of the company rejected in a block because the employees do not feel that they are expressed in practice? Is there an "open-door" policy but no open door? If so, the whole policy structure may be coming under suspicion. Does the official policy say the company exists to render a service to the community when the em-

ployees feel that it is only there to make a fast dollar? If so, either the policy or the practice should be changed in the employees' eyes. If this difference continues to exist, the policies will be shrugged off as window dressing and a general rejection of the company's statements may be started. The key to the accomplishment of the objectives the leader has conceived will be in the degree to which these objectives are seen to be backed up in practice by the Law of Effect on the job.

3. At this point it is necessary to remember the problems that arise in connection with the subordinate's private organization of the world. We must consider the way the situation looks to him, and the way in which his undesirable behavior may flow from a particular organization of the situation. Again, one of the best examples is that of the group of foremen, mentioned above, who treated their subordinates impersonally as payroll numbers instead of people. In this case, line management diagnosed the problem as being seated in the way they saw their subordinates, and led the foremen to collect personal information about the employees which had the effect of changing the way they were seen. In many cases to take effective action depends on this sort of analysis of the problem in terms of the way the other person sees it. It is also well to remember here that the Law of Effect applies to those behaviors which *seem* to lead to reward, not necessarily to those which we may know objectively *do* lead to it. The effectiveness of reward and punishment depends on the way in which it is seen by the subordinate, and the analysis and planning for behavior change should not miss this point. Finally, in considering the way in which subordinates view the world, the leader should question the degree to which present behaviors provide security for the subordinates, and the amount and kind of resistance to change which will arise from efforts of workers to protect this security if the change threatens it. All the

problems of the protective value of the industrial culture and of the individual's security in his own success on the job arise here, and the leader must be aware of them and accomplish his change so that these things are minimally threatened or are replaced with other props in the form of group membership, recognition for achievement, and the like.

4. Once these steps have been taken, the training in practice begins, whether it is formal classroom training at stated intervals or catch-as-catch-can training all day every day on the job. At this stage nothing is as important as the emphasis on consistency that was discussed in Chapter 3. If the superior introduces a policy and then fails to call attention to a violation of that policy, the consistency is threatened. He may feel that he is a generous and understanding boss not to call the subordinate on an action contrary to policy. Actually, the subordinate suffers in that he is now less sure what the policy is. Sometimes if you do it this way the boss jumps on you; sometimes he doesn't. What is the policy? The superior also suffers, in that he loses part of his progress toward shaping his work group in such a way that they will get the job done for him. He is failing to do his job as a superior, and in return for it he is getting the momentary feeling of being a good fellow for having let the infraction slip. Once the policy is started, a consistent application of it is essential to make it understood and to make it work.

5. We have already emphasized the effectiveness of participation in this area, and we shall have occasion to do so again. Certainly the behavior change will progress better if it is possible to elicit participation in formulating the objectives and the ways of accomplishing them. The prethought which the leader devotes to it in step 1 above only prepares him to begin the participative session after having thought the problem through himself so that he knows where he stands on it. If the subordinates have participated in setting

the objectives and the ways to accomplish them, the leader will reap the benefits of their cooperation on the job, as well as their better understanding of it and a more thorough communication of it to the group. It is probably not necessary to go again into the reasons for the effectiveness of participation or the ways to accomplish it. Wherever we look—when we look at motivation, communication, leadership, training—we see the potentialities in well-handled participation, and we have no exception here. Participative consideration of the problems and the remedies will be one of the leader's greatest supports in the process.

6. The leader is now well embarked on his training program designed to accomplish the objectives he has conceived earlier. He finds that all his contacts with subordinates give him an opportunity to put his program into practice. His whole job becomes the accomplishment of his objectives in shaping his work force. In this way he discharges properly the duties of the superior. He is getting help from his subordinates in getting the job done. He is accomplishing production *through* them. He finds that all day, every day, leadership *is* training.

In this list of steps, many of the details of the training program have been left out. Should a group of sessions be planned? On company time? How many people at each? How frequently? Considering the content, what should it include? Economic education for employees? Safety? Job skills? Human relations? In what order should the content areas come? Considering the techniques, should small group discussions be planned? Large lectures? A movie on the company's profit-and-loss statement? Role-playing? Bull sessions? These are the specifics of the training program, and they need to be tailored to the particular situation and the particular job. Moreover, it is a tremendously detailed subject, and one that the leader is not likely to know sufficiently well to decide for himself. It is at this point that the staff expert will be most helpful, in planning the ways in which the objectives will be accomplished, in helping the leader to set it up, and in acting as a continuous consultant on the progress toward its goals.

SUMMARY

1. Training is the leader's job. He is peculiarly fitted for it by virtue of his control of the opportunities for need-satisfaction on the job. The staff man is a consultant to help him, but the leader is the man who must do the training.

2. Within the work group there develop various resistances to change. Many of these are associated with the culture of the group itself, and the leader has a special entry into the group in this sense. He must be aware of these resistances and the kinds of security they represent to the group members, and he must work with them. Part of the effectiveness of participation as a technique for accomplishing behavior change arises from the fact that it is able to circumvent much of the resistance that arises from the culture of the group.

3. The leader's changing of behavior flows either from augmentation of the possibilities for need-satisfaction in his subordinates or from threatening to reduce the need-satisfaction if the change does not appear. In view of the natural tendency to associate authority with reduction in this sense, the leader needs to be particularly sensitive to opportunities for augmentation.

4. Many pressures arising in modern trends in industry put an even heavier load of training on the leader. Particularly the increasing job security, the reliance on seniority, and the deskilling that goes with technological progress all combine to emphasize the importance of the leader's training function.

5. We have seen the relative weight of training and selec-

tion in producing better work on the job. Selection is a great help and a necessary first step. The leader must resist the dream that it will solve his problems and absolve him from the responsibilities of leadership.

6. Finally, the steps in the leader's training program have been tentatively listed. The leader must conceive his objectives as clearly as possible, in his own terms and in the terms of his subordinates. He gets help from the staff expert in formulating them and planning their accomplishment, and then he must take advantage of all the psychological principles in putting them into practice.

□□□□□□□□□□□□□□□□□□□□□□□□□□
□
□
□
□ PRODUCTIVITY
□
□
□ AND WAGE-
□
□
□ PAYMENT PLANS
□
□
□

One of the main concerns of any business is production—
whether it be of goods or services—and the cost of production. Many of our managerial decisions and policies are
directed toward this end, and particularly our personnel
policies, since they are the plans we have for getting our
subordinates to accomplish production. In many cases these
plans and policies involve implicit and unnoticed assumptions about the psychological principles at work in business
—indeed, they should be the practical applications of psychological principles regarding motivation, attitudes, and
behavior change. Since they form such a large part of the
managerial process, and since they are so clearly rooted in
psychological bases, it is perhaps well to consider them in a
little detail at this time.

147

Do we pay for production?

One area in which we tend to be explicit about the psychological underpinnings of managerial policy is in the case of the relation between pay and productivity. Almost everyone would agree that workers are paid for producing, and that superiors in the hierarchy are paid for supervising and producing production. The catch phrase of "a fair day's work for a fair day's pay" continues to hold our attention, with the implicit assumption that we pay a fair day's wages in return for the fair day's work. It is not without difficulties, however. The problem of what, in practice, is "fair" in a fair day's work and a fair day's pay from the point of view of the worker and the payer is the heart of collective bargaining. Even leaning aside from the practical difficulties that arise in applying this maxim, one may very well wonder whether the myth that we pay for production has not nearly run its course. In most cases, what we pay for is attendance, and a minimum of production. Little difference appears in practice in the pay for high production and low production. If a man comes to work on time and stays out of trouble and produces the minimum, he is pretty well assured of his continued pay. If he produces more, in all likelihood, he is still assured of his continued pay. In general practice, we do not pay for production, we pay for attendance.

A whole group of developments in industrial practice combine to work against the idea of paying for production. For one thing, as a plant grows and becomes more and more highly organized technically, the difference in productivity between workers on the same job tends to decrease. As one of the concomitants of routinizing and rationalizing jobs, the situation is built so that everyone works at about the same pace. In its most developed form—in the automobile production lines—there is less than 10 per cent difference between the best and the poorest men at a given job in most cases.

This makes the replacement of turnover easier, but it cuts the ground from under a notion of paying for additional production. Here, as in most cases, we pay for a minimum of production. Pay is not geared to additional increments of production, but rather to the accomplishment of an amount set by very nearly the lowest level. Again, contractual relations have tended to fix promotions and changes of classifications on the basis of seniority rather than merit, and once more the idea of extra pay for extra production is dropping out. In still another example, the tremendous growth in the wage bill in recent years has been in "fringe" benefits, which are not directly related to production but are based on continued attendance and the accomplishment of production minimums as a shaky condition of such continued employment. These extras—pensions, health and welfare, holidays, vacations, and the like—become a sort of fixed charge added to the wage bill which has no relation to productivity, but is simply an overhead cost contingent upon the fact of employment. A rough average of these costs would probably be somewhere in the neighborhood of 25 per cent of the total wage bill; in many cases it runs to 40 per cent. In France, where such developments have gone beyond America's, the cost of fringe benefits is more than 100 per cent—more than the direct wage cost itself. These items serve to underline the fact that our wage payments are not in practice geared to productivity. We pay for basic minimums and do not provide additional reward for increments of production in most cases.

So far we have spoken of pay entirely in dollars-and-cents terms—or, to put it in the words in which we discussed it in Chapter 2, in terms of physical need-satisfactions. This manner of speaking (in dollars-and-cents terms) is surely typical of most managerial statements about the relation between pay and production. We have chiefly intended to equate these two things. By and large, at present, we are not even achieving this equation of production and pay. We should also ask whether we are managing to provide returns in other need-satisfactions geared to the accomplishment of the productive ends of the organization. Do we operate our organizations in such a manner that high productivity will lead to increased need-satisfaction, particularly in the area of social and egoistic needs? To return again to the discussion in Chapter 2, we see the operation of the Law of Effect in this connection. "Those behaviors which seem to lead to reward tend to be repeated; those behaviors which seem not to lead to reward tend to be eliminated." If high production is a kind of behavior which it is desirable to have repeated, it is the responsibility of the manager at every level to see that it leads to reward as far as is possible. We need to survey the extent to which it is true that this kind of behavior does in fact lead to augmentation of the opportunities for satisfactions at work.

We must also keep in mind the third general topic in Chapter 2—the problems that arise in the individual's attempt to make sense and order out of his environment and to answer for himself the question, "What paths lead to goals?" In speaking of the Law of Effect we have again said, "These behaviors which *seem* to lead to reward. . . ." We need to ask ourselves which behaviors *seem* to the member of the organization to lead to reward. Regardless of which ones management has in mind, the principle will operate on the basis of the way the situation *is seen by* those who are involved in it. Throughout we shall have the problem of working within the framework of the world as the worker sees it and of making sure that he sees the rewards as flowing from the kind of behavior that is necessary for the success of the organization and that is necessary for the successful execution of the superior's job. If high productivity and low costs are objectives of the organization, the activity must be operated so that they are seen to be means to the satisfaction of needs for the people involved.

Other things than pay determine productivity—
unit cost is not a simple function of wages and fixed costs

We have suggested so far that we do not provide extra
pay for extra production; pay does not follow productivity.
Let us turn the equation around. There are many opportunities to observe variations in productivity. Do these variations
in production follow variations in pay? If not, what kinds of
variables are associated with variations in production? By
looking at the equation turned around in this fashion, we
may be able to get some insight into the causes of high productivity.

To look at outstanding differences, we often get a kind of
commitment to the job on the part of members of management that is not characteristic of the hourly paid force. Why
do some members of management take work home with them
at night, stay late at the office, spend much of their free time
worrying about how to do things differently and better?
There is a considerable difference in pay between the two
groups, and yet one feels that this is not the causal factor.
It seems unlikely that simple dollars-and-cents additions account for the different kind of attitude toward the work.
Again when we look at the case, mentioned before, of the
worker who does a routine job all day, and then goes home
and sweats blood building a boat in a bottle—exercising extreme care, devising new procedures, and holding the high-
est possible standards for his work—we see the same kind
of difference. Here the financial incentive is reversed. He is
paid for his day's work; he gets no money for the hobby.
Yet in both these cases—the manager and the hobbyist—
there is a kind of motivation that achieves high production.
Much of the difference seems to lie in the way in which they
see the work, in the fact that the work means different things
to them; in short, there are egoistic need-satisfactions present
which are largely responsible for the increased accomplish-

ment. Where are these egoistic need-satisfactions possible on the job?

As we look back over the illustrations that have been used in preceding chapters, or as each of us looks at his experience, it is not hard to find examples where this kind of thing has occurred on the job, and if we examine them we will see some of the things that motivate productivity. We saw one example in the case mentioned above where 100 girls worked together sorting billing slips. When the work situation was reorganized so that they worked in a number of small groups, the quality and quantity of work went up and absenteeism and turnover went down. In the new situation the girls were provided with small face-to-face groups which offered opportunities for social need-satisfactions in the relations with members of the group and for egoistic need-satisfactions in the feeling of being a recognizably important part of the new groups. These incentives seem likely to have played a large part in the new levels of work. Again, in the technological change in the British coal-mining industry, we saw something of the reverse process. The new "long-wall" method of getting coal broke down old small groups and the individuality of functions for workers, substituting for them large relatively impersonal groups and a rationalization of job duties tailored to the requirements of the job rather than the requirements of the people involved. The result was a series of new problems with accidents and absenteeism, and an increase in production that was disappointingly less than had been calculated on the basis of the new machinery, and that made the problem of paying for the technological change doubly difficult. Here we see a deprivation of social and egoistic satisfactions varying again with productivity; this time it is in a negative direction, but the meaning is the same. It has been said, in general, that the increased productivity as a result of technical improvement has only a little more than kept up with the decrease in

productivity contributed by the human factor, so that the
net remains about the same or too slowly rising. One
wonders in how many instances we have a parallel of the
mining case, where the change was designed entirely on
the basis of machinery and resources, neglecting the implications that it had for human need-satisfactions. To take
full account of the value of new methods, they must be
engineered for the operator as well as for the operation.

A variety of experiences with participative plans sheds
still more light on the process. An experiment by Alex
Bavelas provides a good illustration. Working with girls in
a textile-manufacturing production line, Bavelas introduced
what he called "pacing cards." The girls worked on piece
rates on a thoroughly time-studied job with a standard of
60 units an hour and a production of about 75. He held
group meetings with the girls and encouraged them to
discuss their feelings about the job. Then he led them to
make a group decision about the rate at which they would
like to produce the items, giving them cards to set their
goals from one hourly period to the next. These were genu-
ine group decisions and made in the security of an assurance
of average previous earnings regardless of the level of output. The girls' first set of decisions was put at a rate of about
84 units per hour and this was subsequently raised to 95.
The eventual rate stabilized at a figure in the high 80s,
where it remained for the period of several months observed
following the experiment. Here the increase in performance
seems likely to have resulted from providing a certain
amount of autonomy for the girls in the decision, from
egoistic satisfaction resulting from the participation itself
and from freedom from previously felt restriction imposed
by the regimentation of the job. In this case the increase was
met by additional pay under the incentive piece rate in
effect. However, this can hardly be thought to be the
effective factor in raising production, since the possibility of

increased incentive pay had always been present before the experiment.

Many of the so-called "profit-sharing plans" seem to rest on the same base. A labor-management participative committee on cost problems and on procedural matters elicits a kind of motivation that contributes to the productive drive to a large extent. It seems hard to think that the increase is entirely due to the dollars-and-cents return afforded by the profit-sharing features. Indeed, in the occasional case where there are no profits to share because of external market problems, the contribution of participation to efficiency seems to remain. The feeling of being part of a team, of being part of a joint effort, of having a common goal provides powerful motivations at work. The very common wartime experiences where production workers felt themselves to be unusually a part of the national effort underline the same thing. The way in which the worker sees himself and his job holds the key to motivational forces that are probably far stronger in practice than those controlled by pay alone.

In order to accomplish the tasks of management and particularly to guide the formulation of wage and personnel policies to encourage production, we need to see more clearly how the worker sees himself and his job and his pay. We must find ways to operate the organization so that the worker will see management and see the company's objectives in such a manner that they are means to his own need-satisfactions. This is not at all meant to be a sophisticated manipulation of the hourly paid labor force, wherein a false impression is created leading them mistakenly to feel that increased effort is in their best interest. To do this would be both morally wrong and psychologically shortsighted. Such an elaborate speed-up system is insupportable equally on the grounds that it violates honest practice and that it necessarily becomes impossibly cumbersome to maintain.

Rather, it is suggested that, with the objectives clearly in mind, the activity honestly be operated in such a manner that higher production and lower cost *will* lead to expanding opportunities for satisfactions for all the members of the organization. To take a step in this direction, let us look at wage-payment plans in a little detail. Since incentive-payment plans most clearly assert the psychological implications of policy, let us examine them first.

Incentive plans and profit-sharing plans

Incentive-pay plans provide the clearest detailing of the principle of "a fair day's pay for a fair day's work" and the attempt to base the motivation for production solely on financial incentives. In economics and accounting terms, they are sound. The difficulties that they often encounter are largely psychological, and these difficulties go a long way toward helping us to see the way in which pay appears to the producer. In economic terms an incentive system is essentially the same thing as a profit-sharing plan, although the two terms have very different connotations, and those who favor one tend to be emotionally opposed to the other. At base each rests on the proposition that additional units of production accomplished without increased fixed costs raise the margin of return, and the incentive pay is based on a share in the additional profit that is thus made possible. A profit-sharing plan, properly called, usually waits until the profit is realized, but it, too, rests on a base of dividing the increase effected by additional units of production within the same plant. Indeed, except for the time at which incentive is computed, a group incentive is virtually indistinguishable from a profit-sharing system (when "profit" is computed on the basis of labor's contribution to cost reduction). The very fact that the two are similar but that each has its vigorous proponents suggests some of the problem. If the dollars-and-cents pay (and physical need-satis-factions) are the basic motivation to be considered, why is it that equivalent amounts of money returned through either plan do not produce equal amounts of production? Why, in some cases, does a given dollar payroll cost have more effect in the form of a profit-sharing plan than otherwise? A partial answer is that the financial incentive stated baldly is not really describing the situation. We must take into account the way in which the worker sees himself, his work, and his pay for that work.

In many cases incentive plans have become troublesome because the rate of production becomes stabilized at some-thing over the standard rate, and the net pay of production workers tends to be virtually the same at each pay period. When this happens, it frequently follows that the "incentive" character of the additional pay for premium production is lost, and it is seen by the worker to be a part of his base pay. The dollars and cents haven't changed at all, but the mean-ing of this in his organization of the psychological world in which he lives is changing. This is only one of the ways in which the psychological meaning of the pay comes to cut across the "objective" economic motivation. We have al-ready spoken of the fact that individual incentive-pay plans often arouse a conflict within the worker when his group sets a standard of production he can easily surpass. Usually this group-set "bogey" is held to, because the promise of ad-ditional physical need-satisfactions at the expense of depriva-tions in social and egoistic motivations is not sufficient inducement.

In many cases the manner in which rates are installed and policed is such that the economic incentive loses its effective-ness because there is a fear of rate changes. The employee faces the augmentation offered by a possible increment in pay for increased production; at the same time, he faces a potential reduction in opportunities for need-satisfaction, because he is afraid that, if he produces much faster than the present rate, management will try to say the standard is too low. It makes very little difference whether a rate change is contemplated by management. The determinant will be the way in which the situation is seen by the worker. Similarly in the case of another, perhaps equally groundless, fear that is often encountered—the fear of working one's self out of a job. Many industries feel slowdowns of one kind or another because the history of production has led the workers to feel that an increased production rate will only raise the daily level of earnings and decrease the number of days of work. Again, the justification for the fear is not important. If it is psychologically present, it is a determinant of behavior in opposition to the motivation offered by the simple economic incentive. On still other grounds, an incentive rate of production may be felt as a violation of a personal notion of the proper rate of work, and in this sense a threat to the autonomy and dignity of the producer. The rates, both of production and of pay, are not simple variables but are complexly represented in the motivational field and in the psychological world of the employee. The way in which an incentive system will be integrated into the psychological world is an especially pressing problem. By nature, such systems tend to be complicated. They are very seldom properly understood by the recipient. He usually has a general notion that "you get more for more" and that his weekly wage will be about so-and-so much, but he does not have a clear understanding of the details. In speaking of problems of communication we have mentioned the necessity of tailoring communication in terms of the recipient's view of the matter to be communicated rather than in the sender's terms. Also, in discussing technological change, we have seen cases in which the change was tailored to the requirements of the machine and the material rather than to the requirements of the person. Here, again, these two problems come up. An incentive-pay plan is usually built on a rationalized engineering and accounting base, and its essential nature and shape are determined by considerations in these two areas. Beyond this it is usually stated and operated in terms which flow from its origin in engineering and accounting. It typically fails to take adequate account of the worker's view of the situation, of the terms in which it should be described to be intelligible to him, and of the principles under which it should operate in order to take maximum account of his characteristics as well as those of the machine and the material and the process. In all these cases we see clearly that what begins as a simple economic incentive, a simple extension of the "fair day's pay" principle, is in fact a delicate psychological problem because the effective determinant of behavior is within the person and the way in which objective elements such as pay are internalized.

One more important problem must be taken up under this heading. In discussing training we raised the distinction between reduction and augmentation as leadership techniques in getting someone to change his behavior. Essentially, the leader who controls the means for need-satisfaction may create either such a situation that the desired behavior will lead to augmented opportunities for need-satisfaction, or such a situation that failure to produce the desired behavior will lead to a threatened reduction of the means for need-satisfaction. The same distinction applies here, as it does in training and leadership in general, and indeed throughout managerial policy with respect to people. Pay provides one of the need-satisfactions which the leader may augment or reduce. At this point, the distinction can profitably be made a step finer. The leader not only may choose between augmentation and reduction, but in a certain measure has an opportunity to choose the extent to which he will appear personally to the other person to be the controller of the means for need-satisfaction. If the distinction between reduction and augmentation is caricatured as the distinction between "do it or else" and "the carrot held in front of the donkey," the distinction concerning personal involvement is the difference between saying, "If you don't do it *I'll* take care of you," and saying, "The situation is such that if you don't do it no good will come to you." Psychologically this is a big difference. Personal reduction (reductive authority in which the leader threatens personally to bring about the deprivation) is a control by fear. In general human behavior, this kind of control, while effective in many instances, has expensive by-products. It is usually responded to by protective behavior and increased aggression. Protective behavior in response to the "If you don't do it I'll fix you" may take many forms—joining with others to outweigh the leader's control of the means, becoming indispensable to nullify threatened reprisals, or simple withdrawal. Aggression as a natural response to reduction is typified by the phrase "the worm turns." The role of a worm without any control of the situation is intolerable and tends to lead quickly to whatever form of aggression is available. In an industrial situation this may be griping, grievances, work stoppage, or any of a number of ways to strike back at authority. To a large extent an incentive plan often partakes of this kind of personal involvement in the bargain. Although it is not strictly necessary, it often represents an explicit saying, "If you fail to produce so much, I'll see that you get paid less."

To be sure, it also has the personal involvement on the positive side. It says, more or less explicitly, "If you do your part and produce more, I'll do my part and give you more of my money." Even the positive side has its drawbacks in terms of the personal appearance of the leader, however. At its most extreme, personal augmentation is the kind of management that has been recently so much criticized as "pater-

nalism"—the feeling that "I personally will take care of you
if you do the things I like." Where personal reduction is a
control by fear, personal augmentation is a control by gratitude, and it is almost equally difficult to sustain for long
periods. Being under obligation seems to be difficult for all
of us to bear. It is as humiliating and undignified as being
constantly threatened. In self-protection the subordinate is
bound to try to restate the case to himself to show that he is
not getting what he deserves, if only to escape the perpetual
gratitude.

Control by gratitude also has the difficulty that there is no
way to assess what is the proper amount to pay from the
point of view of the worker. If the bargain is expressed in
terms of "You do something nice for me and I'll do something nice for you," there is no rational grounds for deciding
how nice is nice. Such a situation leads to wanting more and
more. If management is going to get into the personal role
of a Santa Claus, it must expect that the presents have to
get bigger and fancier every year. All these examples are
extreme ones to illustrate the point. They all go far beyond
the degree of personal involvement in the bargain which
management usually undertakes, and yet they illustrate in
extreme form the kind of difficulties that arise from such a
system as a base for wage-payment plans. As an alternative,
in order to avoid the unfortunate consequences of this kind
of personal role of the leader in the bargain, it seems quite
possible to operate the activity in such a way that is clear
to each of the members that his role is essential to the success of the organization, that to the extent that he fulfills it
successfully the organization will prosper, and that his
personal prosperity will flow from the organizational prosperity to which he contributed. In this way it is possible to
shift part of the way the worker sees himself and his job
and his pay from the liabilities of the personal reduction
and augmentation. Instead of seeing himself as subject to

fear or gratitude, instead of seeing his pay as being management's tool of control and his job as the testing ground on
which he wins or loses, he can take a different view. He
can see himself as committed to the success of the organization, and his job as essential to the success of the organization, and his well-being as flowing from this success, part
of which he controls. Objectively he is still in the same
situation. Psychologically, he is in a situation where it is
much easier for him to provide help to his superiors in
getting the job done. A great deal of the difference between
what are called "incentive systems" and what are called
"profit-sharing plans" lies in just this subtle difference in
the way the worker sees himself and his job and his pay.
In the one case, management personally controls the pay
and threatens to withhold or promises to grant it. The
reactions tend to be in fear, distrust, outraged dignity, and
apathetic withdrawal. In the other case the worker is an
active participant in something which he has a hand in
shaping, and his return for it comes from the things he did
to make the return possible. For these reasons it seems
much wiser, psychologically, for the leader to stay out of the
explicit bargain in many cases. It is often better to create a
situation such that the subordinate sees that certain consequences—pleasant or unpleasant—flow from the nature
of the situation, rather than one in which he sees the same
consequences flowing from the voluntary decision of the
superior to administer them. This may at first rob the superior of some of his immediate egoistic gratifications in the
situation. It is satisfying to be able to say, "I'm boss here,
and if you don't do as I say, I have the power to make you
wish you'd done it." This gratification is forever lost to the
superior who follows the path of impersonal augmentation
and reduction. In its place he must be content with the
gratifications that come from the realization that he is being
successful as a superior by creating a situation such that his

subordinates help him, and with the eventual recognition from his own superiors as the increased effectiveness of his work group is felt in the organization.

Productivity as a quasi-stationary equilibrium

What determines the rate of productivity? We usually state the problem of productivity in terms of a graph like that shown in Figure 1, where the rate of production is plotted by weeks or months. When we see it fall as it does toward the end of the graph, or when competitive problems put a pinch on costs, we usually ask, "What can we do to

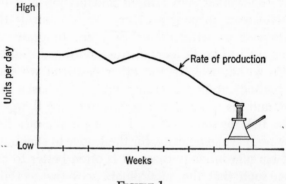

FIGURE 1

raise it? What can we put under the curve to jack it up?" We usually think in terms of a kind of mechanical analogy where we can get under the curve and push it up. The first thought is probably to tell the foremen to watch it a little more closely, and pick up the slack time. The next may well be to deal directly with the producers or with the union, pointing out that production must go up to maintain the economic well-being of the plant. Instead of this approach to the problem, let us suggest two different kinds of questions. In the first place, let us ask not merely, "What can we put under the curve of production to raise it?" but also the other side of the coin: "What is on top of the curve that is holding it down?" In the second place, instead of the mechanical analogy of the jack and the managerial solutions of the foreman's pressure, let us restate the forces in psychological terms. It is just this process of restating the forces in psychological terms and of considering the curve of productivity as a balance of these forces that has been called "quasi-stationary equilibrium."

We often think that one of the things that holds the curve of productivity down is that people are working as fast as they can, that they have reached the physiological limit of the organism. Actually, most industrial production work is probably a very long way from the physiological limit. It would be possible—though not necessarily desirable—to work very much faster. Something else is keeping the curve from rising. I remember once seeing a very rapid hand operation in a paper-manufacturing plant, where girls were interleaving large sheets of paper with thin sheets of zinc to get ready for a pressing operation which would put a pattern in the paper. The girls were working so fast it was hard to follow their hands. I stood and watched, thinking this was surely as fast as possible, and that this must approach the physiological limit. Finally I commented on the speed. The girls beamed and said, "This isn't fast—watch!" and they put on a burst of speed that briefly doubled their rate of output. Two things seemed clear here. In the first place, their original level of production was held down firmly, but not by the limit of their dexterity and physical speed. In the second place, their desire to show me what they could do both added a force beneath the curve of production to raise the rate temporarily, and at the same time temporarily reduced the force that was acting to hold it down. It is this kind of balance of forces and the change in their balance that we need to investigate.

In Chapter 2, in speaking of motivation, we have seen that all behavior is motivated—that all behavior is directed toward the satisfaction of needs. In these terms, we might think of a person as represented by the circle in Figure 2, with a motive and a goal whose achievement represents the satisfaction of that motive. The arrow pushing on the person represents the motive. The rate of his behavior will be determined by the strength of the force and the direction will be

FIGURE 2

determined by the direction of the force. In Figure 3, his hunger remains the same, but here he has to work to get the food. The rate of his behavior is the resultant of the two forces; the speed with which he will approach the goal is diminished. The direction is still the same, since the two forces work in opposite directions; the rate of behavior is determined by the resultant of the two—the longer one minus the shorter one. In most cases, of course, there are many more forces operating on the person, and the rate and direction of behavior are a complex resultant of forces. In Figure 4, for instance, two goals are provided. The direction of behavior (broken line) is determined by the joint action of the two. Often there will be a host of other forces: the person may not want to hurt someone's feeling by not joining him; he may want to be alone to rest; he may want to

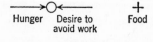

FIGURE 3

eat in company for the egoistic satisfaction of being seen in a particular group. Many such forces are playing on us all the time, and they change rapidly. As we move toward satisfying one need that arises from within us, other new ones arise to change the direction. Similarly, situations change and introduce new factors that call forth other motivational forces, and the rate and direction of behavior is determined by a complex resultant of these forces at any time. We never reach a state where all our needs are satisfied, but are constantly urged on to other goals and other directions by the emergence of new problems and motives.

If we are going to state the determination of the rate and direction of behavior in terms of motivational forces in this way, the problem of production can be translated into these terms. Production is a result of the workers' behavior, and therefore the measure of the rate of production (as in Figure 1) is a statement of rate and direction in behavior. Ideally, we should be able to present it as we have the simpler behavior cases in Figures 2, 3, and 4. However, for this case, it will probably be simpler to think of the pro-

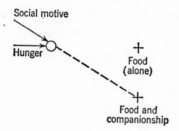

FIGURE 4

duction curve in the terms in which it is usually stated and try to add the motivational forces that are responsible for its particular balance.

In Figure 5 is a curve that might represent a new man learning a task. For purposes of illustration, all the forces tending to increase production are shown as a single arrow, though there are many of them; likewise, the only force shown restraining production is the difficulty of the task, although there are many of them, too. Here the difficulty is great in the early stages (time 1), but the motivation to improve is also great. However, the balance between the two is made at a relatively low level. Later (time 2) the difficulty of the job is less, as he learns about it, and the rate goes up.

As the rate goes up, he is more nearly satisfied with his productivity, and the motivation to improve is less than before. A new balance is made, this time at a somewhat higher level. Similarly at times 3 and 4, the strengths of the two opposing forces are changing. Time 4 may be a stable level at which the difficulty is reduced to a minimum, but the rate is at a level such that the desire to do better is also at a minimum, and for the moment the production curve will stabilize at this level.

Actually, of course, as complex a behavior as production is held in balance by a large group of forces, rather than by the opposition of a single pair. It is difficult to say in general

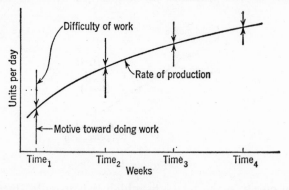

FIGURE 5

terms what particular forces will apply. This will be peculiar to the specific situation, and offers a fruitful field for management to diagnose the forces that are actually operating. Figure 6, however, shows an example of some things which we might think apply. Here the rate of production is shown balanced by a group of forces. The forces are spread out on the line so that we can see them. This makes different ones of them seem to be operating at different times. Actually, all of them (and many more) are operating at any time, but we spread them out here so that we can see them better. As we begin to show the rate of production as a balance of the forces in the situation in this manner, we can change the original question. We no longer simply say, "What can we do to raise it?" We can add, "What keeps it as high as it is?" and "What keeps it from going higher?"

One of the very important effects of this view of the level of production is that it at once becomes clear that it can be raised either by increasing the forces below the line or by reducing the forces above the line. Previously, we have primarily tried to increase production by increasing the driving forces tending to raise it, leaving any restraining forces unchanged but overcoming them by the relative increase. This is somewhat like driving with the brakes on. If the restrain-

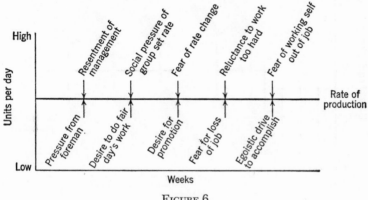

FIGURE 6

ing forces can be reduced, the level will rise of its own accord, until it meets a new balance at a higher level. Figure 7 illustrates the change from these two methods. In the first change, management has, let us say, told the foremen that they have to raise the level of output, and that if they don't the plant may shut down. The foremen increase their watchfulness and pressure, and spread the word that the place will fold unless things pick up. The driving forces associated with these activities increase, and the level goes up until the restraining forces above are big enough to balance the new forces. The resentment of management which previously held production down is overcome, and the level goes up until this resentment again grows. Let us say it was originally a feeling, "Why should I work to put money in their pockets?" Now that feeling is overcome by the fear of losing the job. Production goes up until it reaches a level where the person feels, "At this rate they're making plenty—why should I break my neck to make more for them? It isn't worth it." Similarly with the other forces restraining production. They are overcome until the level reaches a point

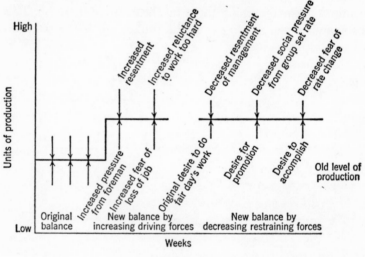

FIGURE 7

where the restraining forces are big enough to balance the increased driving forces and stabilize at a new level.

In the second change, however, a somewhat different change takes place. Here, let us say, management, faced with the same problem, calls for a participative decision on the competitive situation and on ways to increase production and cut costs. Now the resentment of management (restraining) is reduced, and the group pressure against beating the rate is reduced as a result of the group decision. The level of production floats up to a new balance without changing the driving forces beneath it. It goes up until the pressures to work hard, to get promoted, etc., are no longer bigger than the reduced restraining forces. The two techniques have accomplished the same goal—an identical increase in productivity, but with very different by-products in terms of the kind of balance of forces. In the first case it is a balance under high tension, with strong forces on each side; in the second case it is a balance with relatively small forces on either side, under less tension than before the change. This tension itself may have important psychological implications and important implications for behavior on the job.

Probably the simplest by-products of high tension are, in psychological terms, aggression and withdrawal. Translated into on-the-job terms, aggression may mean a variety of things. It may be an increase in gripes about the job, the food, the pay, the conditions of work. It may be bickering with the supervisor, or it may be an increase in grievances filed. Withdrawal may actually be turnover or absenteeism, or it may be a psychological withdrawal that is midway between aggression and physical absence. It is a loss of involvement in and attention to the work that at once protects the worker from the tension and allows him to show aggression toward the work and the management by insisting that the work isn't important to him. The on-the-job specific applications of the general psychological terms of aggression and withdrawal are many and varied and impossible to state in detail. Doubtless all of us have seen a good many cases where just this kind of thing has occurred. A certain amount of tension is probably valuable. It may even provide a motivation to maintain the level, and certainly it will cut down incidental variations in the rate of production. However, it usually happens that an attempt to raise production simply by increasing the driving forces beneath the level without reducing the restraining forces above goes well beyond the useful amount of tension and produces undesirable by-products. In the specifics of their own situations, there is a fertile field for members of management at all levels to look for ways to reduce the forces that hold production down, in order to find alternatives to the present ways to raise it.

It is useful, also, to think of the forces that hold the rate of behavior in balance as extending over the whole field and as varying in strength according to their distance from the balance point. This kind of situation is illustrated in Figure 8. Here, for the purposes of the example, a few points are shown. The first, the difficulty of the work, gets less and less as the number of units per day goes down. At low levels the

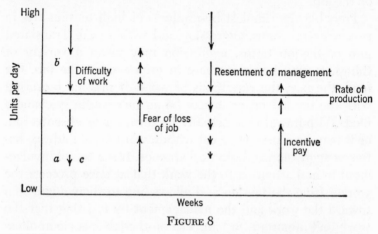

FIGURE 8

difficulty (and the force to reduce output associated with the difficulty) is small (see *a*). At high rates of production the work is much harder and the force associated with difficulty goes up rapidly (see *b*). Similarly with the next pressure shown, that associated with the fear of losing one's job. At very low levels of production (see *c*) there is probably considerable fear, and associated with it a strong pressure to increase the rate. As the rate of production reaches a level that the particular person thinks is the proper rate, the force associated with fear of losing his job drops immediately almost to zero. Two things stand out here: in the first place, the strength of the force operating to raise or lower the rate of behavior changes at different levels of the rate; in the second place, the way in which the strength changes itself changes. That is, in the first case (difficulty) the force decreased evenly as the rate decreased; in the second case (fear of losing the job) the force decreased slowly until it reached the "accepted" level and then dropped off very sharply. In more technical terms, the forces vary as they deviate from the level according to gradients with different slopes.

Financial incentives in terms of quasi-stationary equilibrium

As will be seen from the last item in Figure 8, our thinking about incentive pay for premium production involves assumptions about just this kind of gradient of forces. In practice, the force may be something like the one that is shown. That is, if the rate of production is a little below the incentive level, there is a strong force to raise it. After a certain level is passed, however, there is virtually no force in the direction of earning more. This may be for a variety of reasons. In a Southern mill town it was reported that the girls at the mill told interviewers that more money wasn't any help to them; their husbands took everything over what was needed to run the house. In this kind of situation the incentive pay has no real incentive value in the psychological sense. In other cases, there is a level of pay which a particular person feels is right for him or for the job. He has much less interest in going beyond this level than he does in attaining it. The strength of the force associated with additional pay is not a simple function. Almost certainly, all of us could earn 10 per cent more than we do now in one way or another. However, it isn't worth it to put in the extra effort, or to do the kinds of things that are required. But if it were a question of earning 10 per cent less than we do now, we would go to a great deal of effort to avoid it. The two 10 per cents are not at all the same thing, even though they represent the same number of dollars and cents. They are different chiefly in that they are on the opposite sides of the level which we think is roughly right (or nearly so) and the level at which we have stabilized ourselves. We would do a great deal to avoid a 10 per cent cut. To get us to put forth an equal amount of additional effort, a great deal more than 10 per cent would have to be provided in return. The incentive value to pay about the present level simply is not psychologically the same as the same objective amount below it.

Most incentive-pay plans provide additional pay for additional increments of production. To expect that unit amount of pay will provide a motivating force to accomplish unit amount of production, no matter what the rate of production is, is to disregard the nature of the gradient that we have been discussing. If the desire to earn more money decreases sharply above a certain point, the amount of money we offer must be increased equally sharply in order to compensate for the reduction in the motive. This would mean that for each additional increment of production we must pay, not an additional *amount,* but an ever-increasing factor which multiplies as we go up instead of merely adding. For example, if we were going to pay an additional increment for each addition to the rate of production, we might provide a 1 per cent premium pay increase for each 1 per cent improvement in rate. At this price, it would be possible to afford a 20 per cent increase in production, and well worth the 20 per cent additional wage bill. However, knowing that the money incentive has to be raised by a multiplying factor rather than an additive factor, we know that this bargain won't work. If we pay 1 per cent for the first 1 per cent improvement, we may have to pay 2 per cent for the next 1 per cent improvement, 4 per cent for the next, 8 per cent for the next, and so on. At this rate a 10 per cent improvement would involve a premium pay of 512 per cent! These figures are, of course, hypothetical, but whatever the factor is, it seems clear that we cannot afford to rely as heavily as we have on a simple view of the incentive value of premium pay. Its effect is not a straight line, and as it deviates it quickly gets to the point where there simply is not enough money in existence to pay for improvement.

So far, in considering the psychological problems involved in incentive pay, we have spoken only about the fact that the motivational strength is partly determined by the present rate of pay and rate of production. Another psychological factor arises here, which also works against the incentive value of a simple pay premium. Apart from motivational factors, the amount that must be added to almost any stimulus to be noticed is roughly proportional to the size of the stimulus itself. Thus, if three lights are on in a room, a single additional one may be noticed; but, if ten are already on, the addition of a single lamp may well go unnoticed. In general, the increase in any stimulus which is just noticeable depends on the level of the stimulus to which it is added. With ten lights on we might have to add three to get an increase that was as big as that which was noticed when a single lamp was added to the original three that were lit. Similarly in the case of money, with $100, $10 seems like a real amount; with $1,000 it is less significant; with $100,000, the $10 pales to complete insignificance. On the side of the problem both of perception and of motivation, we find that the human organism is built in such a way that we must provide ever-increasing amounts if we are to command similar-size steps of attention.

This is not at all to suggest that dollars-and-cents pay is worthless as an incentive at work, or that it is impracticable to use as a reward. A long history of industrial practice as well as the motivational background described here would deny this. However, it is an attempt to illustrate some of the difficulties that we get into by facing squarely the implications of a personnel policy based primarily on a financial incentive. These facts should help to indicate that much of management's opportunity for utilizing the motivation of people at work lies in the field of nonfinancial incentives *after* the pay is sufficiently high to assure the satisfaction of basic physical needs.

The role of participation

Viewing productivity in this way not only helps us to see the implications of managerial practices in terms of attempts to raise production and of incentive pay, but also casts new light on the role of participation in the process. It has already been mentioned that participation probably involves additional egoistic need-satisfactions because of the person's individual involvement in the decision. These additional motives almost certainly provide new driving forces acting to push the level up. Participation may also provide more information which helps to set the goal of productive effort more precisely. Most importantly, however, participation provides a kind of group decision, and with it a commitment to the decision which acts to reduce strong restraining forces which keep the level down. In most cases there are a variety of forces—the resentment of management, the fear of a rate change, the group-set level of production, and the like—which arise out of the fact that the two groups, management and labor, see themselves and one another as separate and divided. Consequently the one bands together to protect itself from the other, and out of this divisive view, forces arise which serve to hold production down. Where participation breaks down this divisive feeling, a decision to raise production or to cut costs is not seen as imposed from outside, and there is no need for the feeling, "Why should *I* work harder to make money for *them?*" There is no need for the group to establish and police a low rate of production to protect itself from a possible rate change. The new rate and its means of accomplishment may be seen as "our plan" instead of "their plan," and consequently may not call for the same kind of antagonistic forces. Much of the efficacy of participative techniques seems to come from the way in which it acts to reduce restraining forces preventing a change in behavior.

An ingenious experiment by Lester Coch and John R. P. French in a textile plant illustrates this phenomenon well. In this plant it had been frequently necessary to make more or less radical changes in the work process in order to meet a very flexible competitive situation. Typically, workers who were changed in this manner took a long time to learn the new operation; much longer, in fact, than new workers brought on the job. In addition to their slow improvement, this changed low-production group also typically showed more absenteeism, turnover, and grievances than comparable groups which had not been changed. The experimenters hypothesized that much of the slow improvement came from restraining forces (resentment, group pressures, etc.) arising from the response to the change. Many of the other problems (absenteeism, grievances, etc.), they thought, came from the fact that as the rate approached a higher level in the face of strong restraining forces, it was a balance achieved under high tension, in the manner illustrated in Figure 7. In an attempt to correct these things, an experiment was planned in which some of the changes would be made with participation. These changes could then be compared with similar groups who were changed without participation to see the effect of the two techniques.

One group was changed in the standard manner. The time-study department laid out the new job and set the new rates. The group was called together and given a good statement of the need for the change and its relation to the firm's competitive position. The change was fully explained, as were the new rates, and an opportunity for questions was provided. In general, this method did not seem to be an unfair representation of standard managerial practice in making changes in job content. Other groups making similar changes were handled differently. The need for the change was similarly explained, and they were invited to participate directly in devising the new method and setting the new rate (or to participate by representation, if the group was too large). The changes that were decided upon by the participating groups were essentially similar to the old case, and the rest of the procedure went on normally. As a result of this difference in the technique of changing behavior, however, the participative group recovered their original rate of production much faster than the group changed by the standard unilateral method. Moreover, the incidence of turnover, grievances, and absenteeism was markedly better in the participative group than in the standard method. This example is one of many that illustrates the way in which an analysis of the forces holding productivity in balance at any given time may yield very fruitful insights about what kind of technique will be most effective in producing a change. This particular technique does not necessarily apply to all situations, but it seems very likely that a litle effort spent on the identification of the motivational forces controlling productivity would yield similar suggestions about ways to change.

Productivity and morale

One other psychological factor needs to be examined briefly, the relation between productivity and morale. In recent years there have been a tremendous number of "morale" studies in industry, and there seems to be a general implicit assumption that morale and productivity at least go together, or perhaps that one causes the other. Part of the problem lies in the fact that the term "morale" is uncertain in its meaning. If it simply means enjoying the work situation and having a high positive value for it, there is no necessary relation to production. All of us have seen offices where a group of people had a good time together and liked everything about the job but didn't get much work done. If this kind of satisfaction with the job is high morale, it certainly does not cause high productivity. Indeed, in more careful studies already referred to—those of the Survey Research Center of the University of Michigan—in as diverse situations as the clerical force of a large insurance company and the section gangs of a railroad, most of the things that might be called "morale" did not seem to be conspicuously present or absent in high-production groups. The high groups had about as much job satisfaction and feeling of accomplishment as the lower groups. The simple facts of liking the boss, of thinking highly of the company, do not seem to go with a high level of output. The high-production groups did seem to think theirs was the best group in the company, and it was possible to find different techniques among their supervisors, but even these differences weren't striking.

One of the difficulties may be in the fact that we tend to think that a satisfaction with the job and the way one is doing it, and a general sense of well-being, is morale and that this should be associated with a high level of production. It seems quite possible that in these areas a certain amount of dissatisfaction and a spark of discontent are absolutely essential to provide the initiative to change. If the satisfaction is too smug and bovine, we usually get the common attempt to preserve the present situation. In most human endeavors, better quality or quantity of output seems more likely to be associated with a certain amount of dissatisfaction with the present state of affairs. The problem of morale will perhaps be clearer if we look again at motivation and the Law of Effect on the job.

Productivity and on-the-job and off-the-job need-satisfactions

When we first spoke about the nature of motivation at work it was pointed out that our primary reward is thought of in terms of dollars-and-cents pay, and that this is generally associated with the satisfaction of physical needs. Further, it is in the nature of the situation that these kinds of pay—including vacations, pensions, health plans, and the like—provide satisfactions which can be enjoyed only off the job. The higher-order social and egoistic needs, on the other hand, can in many cases be enjoyed on the job and may well be integral parts of the job themselves. In many cases in practice it seems as though the provision of off-the-job satisfactions has led to a point where the attention of the worker is focused beyond the job itself. It may be focused on quitting time, vacation, or retirement, but it is not on the job. To the extent that we provide rewards which are solely useful off the job, this kind of off-the-job focus seems an inevitable result. The work becomes a barrier which must be endured in order to collect the reward and to have the opportunity to enjoy it. We seem to see people at younger and younger ages picking a job because of its pension plan rather than because of the work itself or what they can do with it. It is as though the glance were lifted from the work at hand to the future after work, or in the summer, or after retirement. Planning for the future is a necessary thing, but if it involves an undue distraction from present production, it is not conducive to a high level of productivity.

In the case of the auto workers mentioned above, it was pointed out that almost all of them liked the job better in their previous occupation but liked the pay better on the production line. In a case like this, where a job with less interest and desirability is accepted in order to obtain something which is relevant only after work, it seems unlikely that the same amount of motivational push is directed toward production. The technological improvement of the job robbed it of some of the values that were inherent in the operation itself. The technical change in this case was great enough to be able to pay more, so that the deficit in on-the-job need-satisfactions could partly be overcome. How much more efficient would it be to combine the technical improvement with an awareness of the human requirements in such a way as to maintain the job-oriented satisfactions of the higher-order needs?

Here again it seems as though one of management's great opportunities lies in the understanding of the on-the-job satisfactions, and the utilization of nonfinancial incentives, not to substitute for dollars-and-cents pay, but to build on basic physical need-satisfactions in the way in which they stand hierarchically. In many ways, management seems to be in the same situation in which flour millers find themselves. We have refined the process of grinding wheat until we have taken out the vitamins and minerals that gave it much of its nutritive value. This seems to have been the necessary concomitant of the technical improvement in the processes of production. The next step has been to supplement the vitaminless excellence of technique by adding the lost nutritive values. In much the same way, the deskilling that has accompanied technological change has taken many of the values that lent work its meaning. Management must look for ways to identify them and replace them. This process seems likely to uncover a real meaning for the relationship between motivation and morale.

SUMMARY

1. In many senses, we do not pay for productivity. A minimum of productivity is expected to hold a job, but we pay for attendance and this minimum. The idea that more work leads to more pay is often violated in practice.

2. The other side of the coin is that we don't get production in return for our pay alone. Other things than pay lead to productivity. In the complex organization of a modern industrial plant, the relation between pay and work is very thin and difficult to deal with. We need to look at other factors influencing productivity.

3. The psychological meaning of incentive pay is not a simple matter. Productivity bonuses of all kinds involve careful consideration. Any such kind of pay plan may raise the problem of the sort of bargain that is struck, with many problems arising from, for instance, an attempt to control behavior by gratitude.

4. It is possible to view the rate of production (or the rate of any kind of behavior) as being determined by a resultant of motivational forces. A more elaborate statement of this shows behavior as being held in a quasi-stationary equilibrium, with several important implications involved in the way in which the equilibrium is modified.

5. The role of participation in modifying any behavior, but particularly productive behavior, is extremely important and capable of more widespread application than is often seen in industrial organizations.

6. An analysis of the kinds of motivation used in wage-payment plans raises the question of on-the-job and off-the-job need-satisfactions, with profound long-term implications for the industrial organization and for the whole society.

CHAPTER 7

ORGANIZATIONS

In the last few years there has been a great increase—both in the United States and all over the world—in the number of firms that have new departments called something like Department of Organization Planning. This development is part of the growing recognition of the fact that the integration and effective direction of large groups of people have become primary tasks of management. The rise of these new departments also leads us to focus on a group of very simple questions intimately connected with the problem of organization in a company.

One of the simplest of these is surely, *"How do you tell a good organization plan when you see one?"* Presumably these departments spend their time preparing several alternative plans and then pick the best one. The interesting question is how to pick the best one. What things are we trying to maximize and what characteristics of the organiza-

181

tion will do it? Beyond this, we might wonder how much it is going to cost us—in a variety of ways—to build one organization scheme rather than another. These thoughts lead us to wonder what it is we're trying to accomplish with the organization plan, anyway, and lead us to the second simple question, *"What are the objectives of the organization plan?"* Finally, as we raise this question, we're bound to wonder what things we have to work with in making organizations of different shapes to accomplish these objectives, and we're led to the third question, *"What is organized in an organization?"* These are three very basic questions that ought to be answered by anyone—at any level of management—who thinks about how to organize and manage his group, whether it is a whole company, a section, or a work gang.

The objective of an organization

A small group where almost everyone knows what everyone else is doing doesn't need much organization. It's when it becomes larger and more complex that the real need for an organization plan is felt. Then it seems essential to recapture some of the *unity* that was lost when the group enlarged and broke apart into smaller units. At the same time, it seems necessary to put some *order* back into the system. When everyone knew what everyone else was doing, lack of order wasn't so noticeable. As the group grows larger, however, it seems necessary to specify functions a little more precisely so that the whole plan will fit together neatly. Finally, it seems necessary to have some *information and control* so that management will have a system for keeping track of what each of the parts is doing. These three things—unity, order, and information and control—seem to be the major objectives of what might be called "classical" organization theory, and they seem to be the major tests for recognizing a good organization plan. "Does it give a good orderly pattern of the whole job to be done with the appropriate information and control to direct it?"

We've left something out, however, and it's something the organization planners often leave out. In addition to the order, unity, and control of the job to be done, we want the *group* to be unified. We want the integration, initiative, innovation, and cooperation of all the people in the organization. This is surely one of the things we want to organize in an organization. Very often, in the past, we seem to have brought order and unity into the job at the expense of the unity and initiative in the people who are doing the job. This becomes more and more expensive as time goes on. One of the things we need to remember when we ask, "What is organized . . .?" is that we want to organize a group doing a job and not just the job. Because a good deal of organization thinking in the past has come from industrial engineers and accountants, the focus has tended to be on the work rather than the people.

A much simpler answer is often given to the question, "What are the objectives of the organization plan?" Often one says, simply, "The best plan is the one that makes the most profits." The simplicity of this is often deceptive, however. It depends on which things we choose to measure— and, importantly, which things we choose not to measure. We usually focus on those things which are easy to measure —budget and production data—and neglect those which are harder to measure—notably the human variables, the degree of integration in the group, the degree of initiative, the extent to which the company's objectives are widely shared throughout the group, and the like. These are valuable assets of the company. If the profits—in budget and production terms—are obtained at the expense of liquidating these assets, they are as unreal as profits obtained by failure to maintain plant and equipment or by the dissipation of any other capital resource.

If a manager takes over a plant, he can show a profit by not replacing raw-material stocks and by cutting down on the maintenance crew and expense. But he will surely be held accountable for these things and his profitable operation discounted as a result. On the other hand, he may take over a plant with a good spirit in the employees, a closely knit group, and a real awareness of the company's objectives. After a few years of profitable operation (in simple terms), he may leave a plant with hostilities and resentments in the work groups, with the employees split into factions or banded together against the company, and with little motivation to produce. He is not held accountable for this resource in the same way that he was for the physical assets. The change in the employees is ascribed to "the spirit of the times," "an act of God," or "outside agitators," and the manager gets sympathy for having had such a hard time. But surely the maintenance of these human assets is part of his responsibility, and one of the primary objectives of the organization plan must be to create human assets, encourage them, and keep track of them. No organization plan that sacrifices initiative in the interest of control can be wholly accomplishing its objectives. No simple measure of profitability that omits the cost to the reservoir of human assets can be a wholly adequate guide to management practice. High among the objectives of the organization is profitable operation in the long run. On the other hand, *the thing that is organized is the group doing the job.* To obtain order and control at the expense of the initiative of this group is not accomplishing the objective. One of the ways to recognize a good organization plan is to see the degree to which it orders and unifies the job and at the same time integrates the group and maintains its productive drive. Both areas must be provided for by the organization plan, and, for the

plan to be an effective tool to help the manager get his job
done, he must be given measures that indicate how well
he's doing in each.

The changing spirit of the times—the concept of authority

A business cannot operate in a vacuum, independent of the
society in which it is imbedded. Business, as a social institution, is part of the society, and its policies and practices
must reflect the values of the society. Questions like "How
hard should a man work?" "How much of himself can we
expect a man to invest in his job?" "What kind of punishments can a company use to direct behavior?"—the answers
to all these and many other similar questions cannot be
found entirely *within* the firm. They depend on the values
of society and on how the people are willing to think of
themselves. If a company's views on these issues are out of
harmony with society's, it may find itself at a competitive
disadvantage. Another company, whose philosophy fits better
with the society's values and the employees' views of themselves, taps reserves of energy that are simply not available
otherwise. In competitive terms, then, a sensitivity to company policy and societal values is essential. In broader terms,
for all of business, it is even more pressing. The very freedom to manage depends on the harmony between managerial and societal values. If business drifts far out of line,
its very freedom to manage its own affairs is at stake. What
sort of values are these and how do they fit in with the
problem of organization?

Winds of change are sweeping the world. They are modifying all our major social institutions—the state, the church,
the educational system, the family. Colonialism is disappear-
ing; new independent nations are growing. Wider and wider
groups of citizens are being enfranchised to vote, and their
standards of living and education are rising. Through all

these changes the broad sweep of history seems clearly to be a progressive change in the role and value accorded to the individual—the Common Man. Business—a major social institution—has largely resisted this change and is organized in terms of concepts of man that were acceptable to man himself 50 years ago.

To see some of these changes, let us ask ourselves, simply, "Why do people do what they're told in a business?" We usually worry more about why they don't do what they're told, but reversing the question will lead us into some of the problems of the changing concept of authority. In general, the answer to the question is that this is part of the implicit contract when a man takes a job. He contributes his skills and effort; the boss contributes the plant and equipment and the pay. The boss owns the plant—or at least represents the owners. When he says "Do it!" there is an implicit "or else"—and that "or else" is "Do it or get off my property!" (or, more recently, "the property I manage for the owner"). We are used to thinking of authority in an industrial organization as being in this way ultimately based in the rights of ownership. The authority to direct with respect to the use of property is one of the rights of property. The authority of the manager comes ultimately from the owner, vested, through the medium of the board of directors, in the president of the company and passed on down by him for day-to-day operation.

This view of the ultimate source of authority is intimately connected with general societal views regarding property rights which have set so many of our moral and legal positions as to what's right and wrong. We've had this particular pattern of thinking for so long that it seems eternal and inevitable. However, this hasn't always been true, and this particular belief seems to be undergoing radical change right now with tremendous implications for business organization.

The primary importance of property rights as a source of authority in business probably began about the time of the Industrial Revolution. Before that, the ultimate source of authority was the state. After the Roman conquests, businesses operated in the conquered territories as concessions. Managers set prices, wages, working conditions, and the like. But they did this with authority granted to them by the state, and it was the state that had to be satisfied with their operation. In return, the state guaranteed (and sometimes delivered) an orderly, safe world in which to do business. Since, in this period, protection was the main requisite, the state, which provided it, was the ultimate source of authority. It isn't necessary to go all the way back to the Roman Empire to see this happening. The British East India Company was a clear example of such a commercial operation depending on the state for protection and power. In extreme cases "gunboat diplomacy"—a show of force making it possible to do business safely—persisted into the twentieth century.

In general, however, except for colonial operations, the need for protection diminished as an orderly society was established. Both in business and in society in general, authority shifted from a coercive authority based on strength to a kind of formal authority working through explicit and implicit contracts resulting from the acceptance of a more ordered society. At about this time, in business, a new force appeared. In the Industrial Revolution, with the growth of machinery and production processes, capital was required to found and pay for the new plants. Taking the state's protection and an ordered society for granted, in the period when capital formation was the most pressing problem, the owner became the source of authority. The "rights of property" became important moral and societal values, and the authority of the manager stemmed ultimately from ownership.

This situation is no longer as true as it once was. In business the *source* of authority is shifting from ownership to the process of management itself. Recently we hear more about "the law of the situation" and the "imperatives of the logic of management." The necessity for a given action seems to flow more and more from the fact that it is the appropriate thing to do. The reason for doing it is grounded in the appropriateness of the action itself, and the authority of the manager, when he says, "Do it," comes less from the fact that he represents the owner than from the fact that the subordinate sees (or has faith) that it is the appropriate thing to do. In this way the force behind the manager's authority becomes grounded in the demands of the job and in the process of management itself.

A group of particular developments have been part of this change, and they have so modified the corporation as a social institution that they are worth looking at in a little detail. The rise of ownership as a source of authority was associated with the problems of capital formation itself. Two progressive changes have been especially important in separating the owner and manager and in diminishing the role of ownership as a source of authority. One of them is the widespread ownership of common stock. As the owners of a company become numbered in the thousands and hundreds of thousands, the "owner" becomes an impersonal, unidentifiable thing. Many company presidents would agree privately—though for obvious reasons it wouldn't be a good thing to say publicly—that the stockholders and the board of directors have nothing to do with day-to-day management. The relationship becomes a simple financial one. Management manages as it sees fit and tries to pay enough dividend to keep the stockholders quiet. Without making it explicit, we are moving to a position in which ownership as such carries with it no right to a voice in management. This separation of the owner and manager, with the focus on the manager's managing, is part of the change that led the source of authority to be grounded in the process of management itself.

The second financial development associated with this separation of owner and manager has been the tendency—since the end of World War II—to finance expansion and product diversification out of retained earnings. The manager no longer goes to the "owner" for new money. Even capital changes are proposed by management in solving management problems and are financed out of the fruits of past management. The owner is largely left out of the decision and is paid off in appreciation of his equity. This internal solution of the problem of capital growth moves further toward placing the source of authority in the process of management. It has another important effect that amounts, in many ways, to a really revolutionary change in the corporation as a social institution. The corporation is cut off from the traditional community check on its practices. In simple, classical, free-enterprise economics, the community can give or withhold approval of corporate growth and product change. As the proposers of change go to the money markets, the community can veto the development by withholding funds. The tendency to finance out of retained earnings cuts the corporation off from the community, and thereby it becomes much more of an autonomous social institution. It forces management to develop a broad social responsibility, as part of management philosophy, and both the breadth and the autonomy put more weight inside the corporation on the process of managing.

One other—nonfinancial—development contributes to the process: the rise of the professional manager. One of the meanings of "professional" in this sense is that the manager feels himself to be a member of a broad horizontal group of managers of many companies rather than the narrow vertical group represented by the company itself. He tends to manage in ways that he thinks other managers would approve of—part of the development of feeling that he belongs to a professional group—rather than focusing entirely on the owner's approval. He feels that his management skills are not restricted to the one company. They are not narrowly related to the particular product or process but, since the process of management extends across companies, are general to the operation of a business. The source of authority is further split off from the owner and more closely tied to management itself.

Finally, in the years immediately after World War II, most companies operated in a tight labor market. Employees came to feel that they could get another job just as good around the corner. In this situation the force of the direction, "Do it or else," was greatly diminished when the "or else" meant "get off the property." As this form of authority diminished, managers had to find other ways to enlist co-operation and direct behavior. They tended to find it in the logic of the production process, in what was clearly "good management." The "Do it" became more often "Do it because it is clear (or you can trust me) that it is the thing that has to be done."

All these things work in the same direction. They cut the source of authority off from ownership and move it further inside the company to the process of management. This internalization of the source of authority is a continuation of the long historical process. When authority was grounded in the state, it rose from something wholly apart from business. As ownership became important, it moved closer, and the grounding in management takes it further inside. It seems likely that we are still in a process of evolutionary change in this development. The ultimate source of authority is moving further and further inside the company to the point where it is grounded in the work groups—at all levels of the organization. It becomes a kind of "consent of the governed." The authority that leads to compliance with the "do it" directive moves to the willingness of the groups themselves. It depends on the integration of the group, the degree to which the objectives of the company are widely shared, and the mutual confidence and trust within all the groups in the organization.

As this happens, as the source of authority moves inside to the work group, a very different situation develops. As McGregor puts it, the ultimate management control becomes self-control—widely spread throughout all the members of the organization. This self-control depends on their commitment to the organization, and the commitment, in turn, depends on their integration into it. The primary problem of the manager—and one of the first requisites of the organization—becomes that of securing and maintaining this integration and commitment upon which effective functioning depends. This development carries with it many specific requirements for the organization, and we shall go into them a little later. First, it is necessary to see a little more of the change in the social context of the corporation and the changing demands that are put on the organization. We leave this first line of change at the point where we see the source of authority in an organization being progressively internalized until it finally arises from all the work groups in the company.

The changing spirit of the times—the concept of man

It is impossible to frame a plan of organization without making some assumptions about the nature of man. We have suggested that classical organization theories tended to organize the work rather than the work group. Even so, since people do the work, it was necessary to make some assumptions about people to suggest how the work they do could and should be organized. One great difficulty is that these assumptions about people are almost entirely implicit. We very seldom bring them out where we can examine them. The result is that we operate with a powerful theory about the nature of man, without ever evaluating whether it is an adequate theory. It is, of course, important to be aware of and to evaluate the ideas on which our policies are based. In this case it is particularly so since the concept of man which is acceptable to society—to man himself—is in the process of change. As standards of living and education rise, job security increases, political freedom and economic independence grow, man's view of himself changes. A theory of organization built on an unacceptable view of man will be much less than maximally effective. It can seriously handicap a firm (or a country) in competition with another organized on principles that the members can readily accept.

Let us look a little at the traditional pattern of organization and see what we can infer from it about the implicit ideas concerning the nature of man on which it is based. Most organization plans have been built on a model that comes from a combination of accounting and industrial engineering. They break the total job down rationally into separate boxes—job descriptions—which are hung on a kind of family tree. Neatness and control are maximized. The job-description boxes are clear and explicit to provide an overview, and they don't overlap; thus there will be a minimum of conflict in the system. A certain amount of authority is put into each box and a certain amount of responsibility is expected out to balance it. Great attention is paid to the detection and control of error. Information systems are built—primarily using budget and production data—to provide a constant check on error and an immediate opportunity to correct it. The parts of the organization exist because one part can't do all the work. Each additional box, consequently, represents a kind of "extra pair of hands" to help get the job done. Usually the job is described so that as little more as possible is demanded of the individual than the extra pair of hands. The people who fill these boxes are assumed to be relatively homogeneous and relatively stable. If we can simplify the job so that anyone can do it, it's easier to hire new people. Once we fill a box, the ideal is to have the man stay there; moving will only upset the system. The traditional organization is essentially centralized and its integration depends chiefly on the authority and control of the central mechanism.

Here, in very brief—and slightly caricatured—terms are some of the main characteristics of a traditional organizational plan. Taking these for a start, what kind of man must they have been designed to utilize? Several things stand out. First, the system is designed to use a man who is essentially lazy—one for whom inactivity is the goal. To deal with this, a careful pattern of incentive, prods, and measures of activity is provided. All of them are external to the person. As little as possible is left to his own initiative and self-starting. The system also assumes that he is shortsighted—not only won't he do anything unless he has to; he won't see that it ought to be done. Consequently, supervision tends to tell him exactly what to do. Self-direction is minimized as well as self-starting. Because they're somewhat narrowly focused on self-interest, rewards, job descriptions, and information are all as immediate and as closely related to the person as possible. He is apt to make mistakes; an error control system is essential. His judgment is poor; judgmental decisions are kept to a minimum.

Here, a little overdrawn—but not very much—are the characteristics of people which can be inferred from the main dimensions of traditional organizations. These aspects of the system wouldn't be put in if we didn't believe people had these characteristics. The policies and practices of the organization are built as safeguards against the assumed qualities of the people who make up the pool from which we draw employees. They are lazy, selfish, shortsighted, liable to error, and are poor decision makers. If we are to use them, we must build a system that allows for these qualities and protects the company against them.

In describing these characteristics, we have said "they" are like this. By "they" we mean, of course, "other people than myself." We tend to see other people as having these characteristics but not ourselves. This is a specific phenomenon of the problem of perceptual organization mentioned in earlier chapters. Our organization of the world may be very different from theirs. Yet as organization planners we often build an organization based on our perceptions and force "them" to work in it. A study done at the University of Michigan illustrates this problem within a company (see table). Workers were asked to rate how important various things were to them on the job. Then their foremen were asked to make the same rating they thought the men would do for themselves. In this way we can see the men's self-perception and the foreman's perception of them. Next the foremen were asked to rate the same items for themselves. Now we can see how their perceptions of themselves differed from their perception of their subordinates. Finally, the general foremen were asked to make the rating the way they thought their foremen had done it and then to do it for themselves.

The three sets of ratings of these things for themselves— by the workers, foremen, and general foremen—were very much the same pattern. On the other hand, in each case the superior's estimation of how his subordinates felt about things was widely different from the subordinate's own. The two groups of superiors tended to see the same things in their subordinates (but not in themselves). In general, socially good traits—interest in the job, willingness to work hard, getting along with others, etc.—were seen as important to one's self but not to the other. If these people were

What Subordinates Want in a Job Compared with Their Superiors' Estimates

	As men	As foremen		As general foremen	
	Rated the variables for themselves	Estimated men would rate the variables	Rated the variables for themselves	Estimated foremen would rate the variables	Rated the variables for themselves
Economic variables:					
Steady work and steady wages	61%	79%	62%	86%	52%
High wages	28	61	17	58	11
Pensions and other old-age-security benefits	13	17	12	29	15
Not having to work too hard	13	30	4	25	2
Human-satisfaction variables:					
Getting along well with the people I work with	36%	17%	39%	22%	43%
Getting along well with my supervisor ...:	28	14	28	15	24
Good chance to turn out good-quality work	16	11	18	13	27
Good chance to do interesting work	22	12	38	14	43
Other variables:					
Good chance for promotion	25%	23%	42%	24%	47%
Good physical working conditions	21	19	18	4	11
Number of cases	2,499	196	196	45	45

SOURCE: From "Human Relations on the Shop Floor" by Robert L. Kahn in *Human Relations and Modern Management*, ed. E. M. Hugh-Jones. Copyright, 1958. North-Holland Publishing Company, Amsterdam. Used by permission.

to plan an organization, a quite different system would have to be built to take care of "the others" than of one's self. The difficulty is that who "the others" are depends on where you ask the question. The organization question is usually asked at a medium-high staff level. "The others" tend to be mainly the hourly paid workers and lower levels of management. They are seen as fairly pedestrian people with rather ignoble motives and serious flaws in judgment and initiative. Consequently an organization plan is built to take care of them; a very different plan would be built to take care of "people like me."

Much of this difference in the superior's perception of himself and his subordinates comes from an earlier era. At a time when there was a big difference in the educational level, standard of living, and social situation of managers and workers—and even between top (owner) managers and lower levels of management—this view was more useful. When a man was more nearly born into a class and level of work, his initiative to do more was less. When he went to work with very much less education than his boss, his ability to use broad information and see general company objectives was much more limited. When his job security and standard of living were such that his constant primary worry was narrowly focused on self-interest, his breadth of vision was less. None of these things is as true today. The error involved in seeing "the others" as essentially different from "people like me" gets bigger and bigger. As these changes in society change the way people are willing to see themselves, several things happen to organizations based on outmoded assumptions about the nature of people. In the first place, the organization fails to take advantage of the initiative, innovation, and commitment that is available and doesn't utilize the productive force the company has. In the second place, "the others," sensitive to a discriminatory demeaning estimation of themselves, develop a positive resentment of the system and the people who framed it.

Finally, organizations tend to create men in their own image. If we treat men as if they are lazy, selfish, and shortsighted, they tend to behave that way. Short-term goals, narrow objectives and information, restrictive job descriptions all tend to produce the kind of behavior the practices are based on. The theory becomes self-validating, and the possibility of seeing more creative contributions to the company becomes less and less.

What would we do differently in an organization based on another concept of man? Suppose we assume that "the other" is essentially like me. In general terms, we would build an organization that used not just the extra pair of hands, but the initiative, innovation, and judgment of the individual. It would maximize participation. In the terms of an earlier chapter, it would create an atmosphere where there is a freedom to make mistakes. While maintaining the necessary safeguards against error, it would permit the individual to try things, to learn, and to take risks. Such a system would assume man to be highly modifiable, and the growth and development of the members of the organization would be one of its major objectives. The integration in a structure of this type would come from a feeling of membership, mutual confidence and trust, shared objectives, commitment, and one group of job skills necessary to operate it. The organization would be, in its essential character, decentralized. Before we go on to deal with specific aspects of such an organization, we should notice that the assumptions about the nature of man underlying it fit much better with the big societal change in the role of the individual and the individual's view of himself.

An organization structure based on the human group

What would the organization be like? The older form was based on a model that grew out of accounting and industrial engineering. It organized jobs and money. A newer form would aim to organize people doing jobs and would be built on the model of the group. Likert has described it well in his book *New Patterns of Management*. The illustrative organization chart which appears in Figure 9 is taken from him. In its basic structure it looks very much like the conventional family-tree type of chart. The important difference is the groups that link the levels throughout the organization. These are the "work groups" of which we have spoken. They are groups not only at the level of the hourly paid worker but at all levels through the structure. They are what tie the organization together.

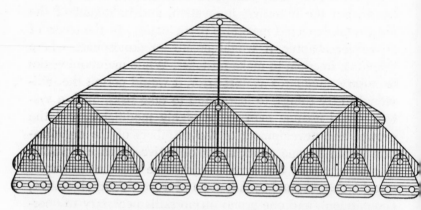

FIGURE 9   The overlapping group form of organization. Work groups vary in size as circumstances require, although they are shown here as consisting of three persons. (From *New Patterns of Management* by Rensis Likert. Copyright, 1961. McGraw-Hill Book Company, Inc. Used by permission.)

In practice, this structure has some real implications. One set of them appears in the job of the superior at every level of the hierarchy. His first responsibility is to make sure that a group does, in fact, exist, following the diagrams illustrated on the chart. His second responsibility is to make sure that he is a member of the group. It very often happens that a man's subordinates form a closely knit group, part of whose defining character is that the boss isn't a member of it. This kind of development tends to create a series of autonomous little cliques not integrated into the company's objectives, whose group structure lends strength only to factionalism or to counter company policies. If there is no group, we have a series of individuals without integration. If there is a group and the superior isn't a member, we get factionalism and organized resistance. Consequently the superior's first two jobs are to see that a group exists and that he is a member of it.

The third job—and one of the defining characteristics of the superior at all levels—is to see that he is a member of the group above him—the group in which he is a subordinate. It also often happens that strong, almost impenetrable, horizontal layers develop in the company. This occurs when the superior creates a group below him and belongs to it but not to the one above him. He often does this by saying, essentially, "I know it's a silly rule, but *they* say we have to do it." This technique of joining the group below by fostering or approving a common rejection of the group above is seductive and attractive. On the other hand, it makes the organization of the whole structure completely impossible. The horizontal layering makes communication difficult and impedes any sharing of objectives between levels. This creation of an impersonal "they" to blame for things we don't like is also often supported by higher levels. In the absence of good vertical integration, higher levels tend to take the position, "They don't understand what we're trying to do." Thus each group is equipped with a comfortably inclusive "we" to belong to and an impersonal unconnected "they" on whom the blame can be shifted. This layering of the structure is probably the commonest fault in organizations. It occurs when the supervisor has not assured himself of his three basic functions: creating a group, being sure he's a member, and being a member of the group above. Each of them is important, of course. Together they make up what Likert has called the "linking-pin" function of the supervisor's job—being simultaneously a member of the groups above and below him.

Notice that a large part of the job of each member of the organization has already been specified without saying anything about what he is supposed to do in terms of product or process. It is in this sense that the organization is designed to organize people so that they can do a job, rather than to organize a job that has been rationalized and fragmented into bits in job-description boxes. Once this first group-structure step in the organization is assured, the job content and managerial practices fit naturally, as we shall see later. Unless the group is built, however, the job itself is not a very effective medium for integration.

The task of building this group structure is by no means easy. The company may need to stand ready to provide specialized training to help accomplish it. Everyone in the organization, as has been pointed out before, needs not only job skills to do the work, but group skills to make the organization work. In this latter area particularly we may need some special help. We probably need to provide some training in group leadership and in group membership. Most companies are used to leadership training but not to membership training. We used to think that leadership was a quality that was born in the person. Now we realize that we can and must develop it where it is needed. Similarly, most of us feel that we know how to be group members. Haven't we been members of a variety of groups all our lives? However, the task of being a good group member is not easy and cannot be taken for granted. It is possible to train people to become sensitive to the role they habitually take in groups—the silent-summer-up-later, the "let's define our terms" obstructionist, the you-go-your-way-I'll-go-mine isolate, and a host of others. It is also useful to see the action of specific behaviors on such things as group-building processes, objective setting, morale raising, and the like. Considerable help can be provided in these areas of group building and group membership. In addition, the company, to implement a good organization plan, must support it with training.

Beyond these tasks, the group leader has some other responsibilities that begin to come closer to the actual work of the company. First, he has built the group, and it is partly from this integration that the commitment comes. However, the commitment must be to goals and activities as well as just to the group. Now the "linking-pin" function becomes important in action. Between the two levels the leader carries the information and objectives until he can assure himself that he has widely shared objectives in the group below him and that they fit into the objectives he shares as a member of the group above him. As a leader of a group he takes part in setting objectives, making plans, and considering possibilities. As a member of the higher group he reports these goals and capabilities there. Here, too, he takes part in setting objectives—realistically, now that he represents the agreed capabilities and goals of his subordinates. He shares this information with the higher group and also information which the leader has brought—in a similar process—from still higher groups. Finally, he reports all this back to his own group to share the information there and, if necessary, reset their objectives. The new objectives will have been suggested above in the light of known expressions from the lower group and the modifications will be accepted only to the extent that they fit the group's own knowledge of its capabilities, the information it has, and its own objectives. This ability of the lower group to influence the upper group's decisions and policy making is an essential and will be discussed further in the next section.

The leader performs this "linking-pin" function of going back and forth between groups, carrying information both ways, and resetting objectives at both levels a dozen times a week or a day. With all this to do—build a group, belong to another, run back and forth between the two of them— one is tempted to say, "But when is he ever going to get his job done?" The answer to that is clear: This *is* his job. In discussing leadership, we pointed out that the superior is in a superior position because he is responsible for more work than one man can do. That's why he has sub-ordinates to help him get it done. His job is not to do the work but to create a situation such that they will help him to get it done. This is a good description when we are discuss-ing the individual's leadership role. When we turn to the organization problem and the task of fitting each leader and his group into the complex whole, it is just this "linking-pin" function that *is* his job. This is what creates the fabric of organization. This is what is organized—not the job. The structure is provided in this way to carry job content and information about the work up and down. The organization is in the group, not the job. The organization of the group makes the job possible.

The human group model—expanding influence

In discussing the "linking-pin" function, we spoke of the fact that the lower groups influence the objective setting and policy making of higher groups. It is time to go into that in a little detail now. The point is clearly related to one we brought up earlier—the changing concept of authority and the tendency for the ultimate source of authority to be grounded in the work group. It is just this kind of work group that was meant and the operation of the authority de-pends on an extremely important principle: *The amount of influence a superior has with his subordinates depends on the degree to which they can influence him.* Put differently, it means you can't have any influence down unless you can influence up. The influence—or authority—comes from the mutual confidence and trust of the group, their shared information and objectives, and their integration and commitment. This comes because the subordinates *did* have the information and took part in setting the objectives, because they *are* a group and the leader is a member. He has confidence in them, as group members, to take part in setting and carrying out objectives. They have confidence in him—in his role as member of the higher group—to carry up the information about their capabilities and willingnesses and goals and to fit them into the objectives set at that level. Unless he can do this—and unless he can take part in and influence decisions at that level—he can't operate effectively at the lower level. He loses his ability to influence his subordinates if he can't influence his superiors. In that case he would have to fall back on coercive authority and the threat of dismissal, and the initiative of the group and the strength of the organization would be lost. The key to the successful operation of the organization is exactly in the linking-pin. It must be a two-way channel for influence as well as for information.

One somewhat startling and important phenomenon develops out of this kind of authority. There is reason to believe, from recent studies, that the total amount of authority in the system is capable of being expanded. The amount of influence is not a finite pie, to be divided up into appropriate slices, but can be increased. Conferred authority—the kind that is bestowed upon a job in the traditional organization—is necessarily limited in the total amount. The other kind of authority—of which we have been speaking—is accorded to the leader by the group. They can give more or less of it, and he can make much more authority than can ever be given to him by the centralized head. This has important implications for organization structure and practice. One of them is to allay the fears of the person who is afraid that giving his subordinates a participative voice in decision making and objective setting amounts to an abdication of his job. On the contrary, it becomes clear that giving the subordinates more opportunity to influence the superior actually *increases* the degree to which he can influence them. Not only do you have no influence down if your subordinates have no influence up, but, in general, the more they can influence you, the more you can influence them.

This has another important aspect for the size of the growing organization. One of the sticking points in growth is always the decentralization of authority. When we think in terms of a traditional concept, with conferred authority flowing from a centralized head, there is a real limit on expansion. When the authority stems from ownership and is vested in the chief executive officer through the medium of the board, it is a finite amount. The big boss is given the authority to manage. As he gives out subsidiary concessions to manage parts of the company lower down, he breaks off a piece of his original authority and confers it on the decentralized responsible man. At the same time, in such a system, he must retain enough of his original authority to keep a kind of majority voting control. In a sense, he has to keep 51 per cent of the total authority. As the job is further decentralized, similar small chunks of authority are broken off and passed down, always keeping an overriding amount of authority at each higher level. Eventually, a real limit to possible expansion occurs when the amount that must be retained is so great and the amount that can be passed down is so small that further decentralization is impossible. The limit to growth comes from the finite initial authority, the necessity of keeping working control, and the idea of conferred authority. On the other hand, if the authority arises from the work group and is capable of expansion, the limits to growth disappear or recede into the far distance.

This description slightly restates the limitation on growth

suggested by the economic theory of the firm. There, usually, the suggestion is that diminishing returns occur with growth because—owing to the triangular shape of the organization—there is only one man at the top of the company. He is a finite commodity in the company, but because the industry may have a large number of similar competing companies, their chief executives may be a virtually infinite commodity. Consequently, a single firm will feel the pinch of overloading the top officer while all the other, smaller firms spread the load among their many heads. Thus the diminishing return from increased size comes from the finite scope at the top of any one firm. Usually this finite commodity at the top is described as the decision-making capacity of the chief executive officer. When this is fully occupied, further growth leads to diminishing returns. But surely he can delegate decision making to subordinates as long as he retains an integrated organization with shared objectives and information. If his influence can be expanded to embrace the larger system, the point of diminishing returns with growth can be pushed further and further ahead.

One more point arising from this expanding authority seems worth a moment's notice. The basic idea is that if one gives up some of his formal authority by allowing subordinates to influence him, his total influence is not diminished thereby but actually increased. The same thing seems likely to be true in relations between groups. If one group joins a group or groups and gives up some of its independent authority to make decisions, it is not necessarily impoverished by the process. Its influence may, similarly, be increased. Nations which avoid multinational organizations in the interest of preserving sovereignty seem to be hoarding the same kind of finite conferred authority at the expense of an increasing authority accorded by the group. Companies that insist on "going it alone" seem to represent another expression of the same view of a unilateral authority that comes from concentrating on what you have rather than the kind that arises from the consent of the governed. The ramifications of this kind of view of the organization and its processes are remarkably broad.

Specific differences in the two views of
organization authority and responsibility

In more specific terms, what kind of things would happen differently in such an organization? A good many. First, the changed view of authority immediately comes in contact with one of the most frequently repeated old wives' tales in organization theory: the idea that authority should be commensurate with responsibility. A whole group of problems seems to arise on this issue. First, the statement requires a special, outmoded view of both authority and responsibility. Second, there seems no reason to insist on the equivalence of authority and responsibility. Third, it seems virtually impossible to maintain the equivalence in practice. Fourth, it seems an unnecessary hangover from the accounting tradition in organization theory. Finally, it comes into sharp conflict with some other sacred cows in organization jargon. Let us look at each of these points.

The statement that authority should be kept commensurate with responsibility (or vice versa) is almost always found in textbooks on management and organization. *Why* it should be so is not explained. It seems to be one of those myths that is repeated so often that it is unquestioningly accepted without inquiring about the reason. In no other sphere of one's life is authority commensurate with responsibility. Why should it be so in business? The citizen's responsibility far exceeds any authority he has. So does the neighbor's, the church member's—almost every group to which we belong. Perhaps clearest of all is the parent's case. His authority seems to be least just when his responsibility is most. Why, in this one special case, should the two be so carefully balanced? The argument seems to be that it is not right for a man to be responsible for something over which he has no authority. But it is just here that the special meaning of the two terms seems to arise.

If by "responsibility" one means that a man is completely answerable for the success or failure of an operation—that he will be blamed if it does not accomplish the objective—then, to protect himself, he must limit the responsibility he accepts to those things over which he has a direct and immediate control. But this narrow sense of responsibility cannot be the kind of thing we hope every member of the organization will feel. Surely we want him to feel a responsibility for broad objectives and general goals of the organization. We want him to feel responsible for creativity and innovation and things that were never described in his job. We want him to feel responsible for doing all he can to accomplish the objectives—not to feel that he can safely accept responsibility only for those things that can surely be done. Narrow responsibility shows up often in practice (and at great expense) when someone says, "I did what I was told; if it wasn't the right thing, it's not my fault." "That's his job; the reason I didn't do it is because I'm not supposed to." These attitudes cost companies immense (and unaccounted) sums in things not done or not done right because they're "not my responsibility." This meaning of the term "responsibility" is a long way from the feeling of general commitment to the organization which is a major goal. The narrow definition is part of a long tradition of evading responsibility by circumscribing responsibility that stretches from Pontius Pilate washing his hands of Christ's sentence because it was taken out of his jurisdiction to the generals who explained away war crimes by saying they only did what they were told. We can't afford narrow responsibility in a company or in a society.

A special meaning is necessary for "authority," too. Only formal conferred authority can be graded and defined in these measured units. The authority that arises from the group may be increased tremendously by leadership practices. Much more influence is available in the service of discharging responsibilities as one uses the personal authority that arises from his membership in the group and from their shared objectives. Just as the narrow definition of responsibility worked against organizational goals, the narrow definition of authority unnecessarily commits the organization to a specific and less than ideal concept of authority.

Beyond the limitations in authority and responsibility that the balance principle gets us into, there is the problem of how to do it. How do you make authority equal to responsibility? If he has more responsibility he should have more authority. How much more? In what kind of units should the authority be measured to tell us how much more authority should be given? These questions seem impossible to answer. Suppose a salesman has a given territory and, initially, presumably an authority commensurate to this responsibility. Better transportation and better communication make it possible to handle a bigger territory. He has more responsibility, so he should have more authority. But how much more? Well, first we need to know how much more he is responsible for. How do we measure it? The geographical size of his territory? The dollar volume he gets or the dollar volume he could get? The number of customers or the potential number of customers or the amount of competition he has to face? It seems very difficult to compute the quantitative increase in responsibility in order to fix the appropriate amount of authority that must be added.

The authority is easier to handle, at least on the surface. We are used to the idea of commitment authority. Such a level has the authority to commit so and so much money without prior review at a higher level. Now if we want to double authority we have at least a convenient scale for measuring amounts. We just double the number of dollars he can commit. However, this authority to spend is, we hope, a very small part of the authority he uses in doing his job. The rest is left untouched. Moreover, every experienced manager knows how to go beyond the intended authority by repeated commitments. On both sides of the equation the calculus seems virtually impossible.

The idea of the balance in the first place seems to have come from accounting practice, from the desire for a neat, orderly system, and from a desire to keep most of the drives in the system external to the individual. If we can give him authority and responsibility, we retain control at the top and we know at any moment how much there is anywhere. If he can expand (and contract) his feeling of responsibility depending on managerial practices, it is much less neat and arouses much more anxiety. Now the top manager is responsible not only for running the company, but for the very feeling of responsibility that his subordinates have. Similarly with authority: if the subordinate manager can increase his personal authority by the way he handles his work group, we need a quite new measure to know how the system's functioning. It is no longer the neat circumscribed structure we drew on paper. The accountants had set up a nice double-entry bookkeeping system that doesn't work any more. They drew authority from the top and put it into the subordinate's job. They expected responsibility from him in return and they credited it to the general company account. If the subordinate increases the authority and responsibility he has, it's as bad as printing more money; the books will never balance. This kind of input-output accounting model may be a good way to keep track of cash flow, but it's a poor system for regulating the operation of a human group where the variables are drives and commitments rather than dollars and cents. These are properly psychological variables and as such they arise from within the individual; they are not put in from outside in nicely measured amounts. The task of the organization plan is to create a situation that will nourish and expand these drives, not to circumscribe them unnecessarily and unrealistically.

Finally, if we persist in maintaining the commensurate character of authority and responsibility, we must eventually deal with that other hoary old institution in organization mythology: the separation of staff and line. In its frequency of repetition in textbooks, it is probably second only to authority and responsibility. It is constantly repeated that the staff's function is to provide advice and support to the line. It persuades on the basis of its expertness in its specialized function. It has no authority to put its point of view into practice. The authority belongs to the line—the "line authority." If we put these two notions together we reach a strange conclusion. If the staff has no authority and we maintain a balance between authority and responsibility, surely it follows that the staff has no responsibility! But no organization plan ever envisaged this. We just keep the two concepts simultaneously by maintaining them in logic-tight compartments while we think about the organization.

Again, the problem seems to be in what we mean by "authority" and "responsibility." The staff's persuasiveness arose from its expert understanding of its specialized function and its ability to point out that if we want a certain goal we must take certain actions to reach it. The line, on the other hand, had the "do it or else" authority. But the staff's persuasiveness arising out of expert knowledge sounds more and more like the line manager's "law of the situation." The line manager progressively gives up the "or else" and his persuasiveness arises from the process of managing itself—from the fact that what he asks people to do is seen or believed to be the appropriate thing to do. The two kinds of influence come closer and closer together. Staff and line "authority" become indistinguishable. It's probably time to stop trying to distinguish them. Certainly in practice one company has differed from another so much in what it considered staff function that the distinction served very little useful purpose. Very little seems to be lost by giving up the distinction between the two. If we eliminate it, along with the idea of commensurate authority and responsibility, we can leave the expensive circumscribed responsibility and the narrow conferred authority and go on to a more fruitful concept of broad commitment and expanding influence grounded in the participation of the work group.

Information and managerial control

When Field Marshal (then General) Montgomery took over command of the Eighth Army in the desert in World War II, he postponed a major battle that had been fully planned. All the logistical and tactical preparations were complete. Montgomery postponed it long enough to talk himself with all the officers about the battle plans and to have them talk with all the men. He said, "If every unit commander knows what is wanted, then all will fight more intelligently and cohesion will be gained. . . . Every single soldier must know, before he goes into battle, how the little battle he is going to fight fits into the bigger picture and how the success of *his* fighting will influence the battle as a whole. The whole army then goes into battle knowing what is wanted and how it is to be achieved." The ideal expressed in this is one most people would agree with, and most companies would piously second it. The important thing is that Montgomery recognized its importance sufficiently to postpone the battle to build this integration. Like many personnel practices, the commander before him probably agreed with the principle but neglected the practice. Later, when Montgomery was made Commander of Allied Ground Forces in preparation for D-day, he insisted, similarly, that he must talk to all the officers and they to all the men. It was protested that this involved some six and a half million men. Montgomery realized that the large number only made the shared objective more important. He insisted on, and accomplished, the tremendous task of visiting every unit and talking to all officers. Many companies could profitably learn from this example. The investment—and even risk— involved in sharing information and objectives may be considerable. The return, in terms of cohesion, integration, and commitment, makes it essential. It is, unfortunately, easy to omit the step and then blame the rest of the organization for not having the company's interest at heart.

The newer organization structure would suggest a quite different routing of much information. Typically, today, budget and production data are generated by the action of groups at the middle and lower levels of the company. This information then goes immediately to the top to a centralized control. Here it is used almost entirely as a check on error and as a punitive weapon to chastise groups which have fallen below the mark. The first thing the group which produced the information knows about the results of its activity is when a superior descends, brandishing a summary, and complaining about the lack of performance. Budget and production data are not made available to help people solve their problems but to strengthen the centralized top control and to act as a prod and error control. In using the linking-pin structure, such information would appropriately go to the group which produced it. They could discuss why it was what it was, restate their objectives and modify their practices, and the leader, in his linking function, would carry it up. In this way the information would be used to guarantee shared objectives and solve problems rather than to centralize management control and provide a punitive weapon. Of course, while the major part of the information was being fed back into the system at the level which produced it, a certain amount would be siphoned off and fed to centralized levels for long-term planning of capital investment, production plans, marketing strategy, and the like. These are the functions appropriate to these levels, which need the information to perform them. It is injurious to the organization, however, when the information is centralized to strengthen managerial control.

The development of electronic data-processing equipment sharpens this question for organization structure. We have been reaching a point where sheer size has forced the decentralized dissemination of information. Now the speed of modern information systems offers a sharp alternative. Will they be used further to centralize information and management control, or will the same qualities of speed be utilized to provide the outlying parts of the organization with more information faster? The two possibilities face many companies clearly just now. One of them can be used to build and strengthen the organization. The other is designed to perpetuate an outmoded managerial technique.

Performance Evaluation

Much of performance evaluation in the past has followed the same pattern as the handling of information. That is, it has been a centralized unilateral tool for control. It has been something that "happened to" the subordinate rather than something that he took part in. Even though he produced the performance that was being evaluated, it was not available to him as a problem-solving, objective-setting tool. The performance was evaluated and the evaluation presented to him. Perhaps he was even asked to sign it. But it was not part of *his* evaluation and not maximally part of his opportunity to learn and grow.

If, instead of this, the superior and subordinate meet at

certain intervals for an explicit joint formulation of the subordinates' objectives, the situation can be radically different. At the next meeting, the subordinate has all the information about his performance and groups. He knows to what extent the objectives set were realized and to what extent they were unrealistic. He and the superior can, jointly, evaluate the performance and, jointly, set new objectives for the next period. The situation is now very different. The objectives are *his;* the performance is *his;* even the evaluation is *his.* All the important steps come from within the individual instead of being applied to him from outside. The drive in the system is internalized and relies on individualized initiative, rather than being externalized and relying on centralized control. At the same time, the individual, sharing information and objectives, becomes an integral part of the system and the necessary base is laid for the commitment which leads to his self-control.

Executive development

Closely related to this is the problem of the growth of managers. If one asks a group of chief executives what are the qualities in which their potential successors are most deficient, the answer is seldom in closely job-connected skills. The answer tends to be that they lack breadth of judgment, the ability to grasp all the relevant information about a problem quickly and take a well-calculated risk successfully. They lack the ability to set objectives wisely, broadly, and creatively. They are not as strong as one would like in organizing a group to accomplish objectives or in leadership. When we look at the jobs of most middle managers, it is no wonder that just these qualities are lacking. Most middle managers' objectives are largely given to them; the opportunity for planning is largely confined to the routine of schedule setting, assignments, and the like. The information that is available to them is usually incomplete, so that new creative solutions are either impossible or off the mark. Their opportunity to organize the group is largely inhibited by the structure of the organization, and in any case, this variable is seldom mentioned in their performance evaluations. All these things being true, it is not surprising that these are the qualities that are lacking in successors-to-be. If we want these qualities in managers, we must give them jobs that allow them to grow. If we want executives developed, we must develop them. Their job and their superiors will be the chief factors in this development.

McGregor has spoken of the various approaches to executive development that organizations tend to take: the "sink or swim" model in which a group with high potential is hired on the theory that those who survive will be executives; the manufacturing model, in which the assumption is made that if we want certain behavior in executives, the thing to do is build a training course that will mold them that way. Finally, there is the agricultural model in which executives are nourished and tended and encouraged to grow; but the growth comes from within them, and the organization's job—like the gardener's—is to create a situation where they can grow. If we want to grow executives, we must provide them with information so that they can conceive objectives broadly, take risks wisely, and organize accomplishment creatively. All these things belong in the joint objective setting with the superior, and then, later, in their joint performance evaluation. At this step, the development of these qualities becomes really a part of the man's job. As long as the evaluation is based primarily on routine production, routine production is the main characteristic of the job.

In recent years it has become fashionable to emphasize the decision-making aspect of the executive's job. Many executives welcome this because it glamorizes the job. It gives them a kind of Solomon-like role of rapidly marshaling all the relevant facts, making lightning judgments that cut to the heart of the matter, and steering the destinies of the organization like that romantic figure the ship captain. A delightful dream! But, unfortunately, not very true. To be sure, there are crucial timely decisions that change the whole course of a company. But they are rare. Decision making occupies a tiny fraction of the executive's day. Even in decisions, a very large number of them make themselves. As the facts are gathered and the possibilities weighed, the facts themselves force a decision in many many cases, almost without the intervention of a human agency. Further, most companies have a kind of internal logic in the process that means it must go in certain ways—no decision is necessary. Indeed, in many cases, if no one made high-level decisions for several months, everyone could come to work normally and do his proper job and no one would notice. The inertia of the process could carry it on. On the other hand, if no one took any steps to hold the the organization together for several months, the result would be a shambles. Here is the real heart of the manager's job and something he should put high on his job description. His responsibility is to see that the organization doesn't fly apart in all directions at once.

Whenever anyone joins a group—any group—he gives up some of his individual freedom. In any group—a family, a church, a country, a company—the member's behavior is constrained somewhat by membership. If he is to remain a member, he must accept to some degree a modification of personal goals and inhibitions of personal behavior tendencies to accept group goals and group patterns of behavior. He gives up these things, presumably, because in the group he finds opportunities for satisfactions and accomplishments that would be impossible alone. This is the return for the sacrifice of individual freedom. But it is always an uneasy contract. The group is made up of individuals, and as such they still retain a tendency to fly off on their individual paths to goals and satisfactions. This centrifugal force arising from the individual is probably the most potent force threatening to destroy the group. In organizations a constant job is to counteract this tendency to fly off the group path. The manager must be forever binding the group together and seeing that they have common objectives. This takes a lot of time and it's what most managers should be doing with a large part of the time that they're not making decisions. Because this threat to destroy the organization by making it fly apart into its components is so constant and so potent, resisting it needs to be a high-priority job. The evaluation of performance should take this accomplishment into consideration, too, to fit it into the job. The development of the executive should both emphasize this function and provide group skills and organizational tools to accomplish it. Otherwise the organization will degenerate, entropically, into a disorderly collection of individuals.

Promotion

Promotion is, of course, part of both performance evaluation and executive development. It is a sign of the evaluation of performance and as such encourages certain sorts of behaviors. It is part of the career development of the manager, and, again, tends to emphasize certain sorts of behaviors. As such, it demands especially clear thinking in its application, and these are particular pitfalls connected with each of these two aspects of the operation that threaten the vitality of the organization.

We have already spoken, in another section, about the tendency to promote on the basis of seniority rather than merit. Where the union contract applies, companies often avoid arguing the issue of relative merit, promote for seniority, and thus build into work groups a tendency to expect reward for longevity rather than productivity. At middle levels of management a somewhat different, but equally difficult, phenomenon occurs. Promotion often seems to be based on a kind of rough sense of social justice. "Old So and So deserves the job. He's performed long and faithfully in the lower level. He ought to be moved up." This kind of long and faithful service certainly does deserve reward. Whether it deserves promotion is quite another question. The whole organization deserves to have a promotion filled by someone who can do the job well, not just by someone who has done another job a long time. The idea that social justice demands that long service be rewarded by eventual ascent seems to be a strong value that works just below the surface of many personnel decisions.

It is a truism to say that a job should be filled by the man who can do that job well—not by the man who has done some other job brilliantly, as in the case of the star salesman promoted to be a bad sales manager; nor the man who has done a routine lower job so long that he deserves a reward. It is too true to need repeating, but practice demands it. Particularly in large organizations where the cumbersome anonymity of large numbers enables people to hide in the crowd, promotion policy often stifles managerial development. The surest way to advance is to be around a long time and never do anything wrong. Risk is minimized. Organizations seldom pay off for risks successfully taken and they fairly surely punish the risk that misses. The path to success becomes staying out of notice until your time comes. The result to the organization is often a gradual drifting to the top of a group of people unfitted for top leadership. The qualities that were responsible for their advance are irrelevant to or antagonistic to the demands of the job. To develop and have available successors to the whole top group of jobs, the promotion practice needs to be carefully scrutinized.

Many companies also think in terms of a man working his way through a series of jobs to top-management levels. This is a variant of the argument from social justice. It is a little like the idea that you must eat your spinach before you can have your ice cream. There are a lot of dull routine custodial jobs in the company. The tradition grows up that everyone must serve his time in them. The rationalization is often that he must "learn the business." But if the candidate requires several years in one of these jobs, he clearly isn't the caliber for top management anyway. The jobs often require, for example, primarily the careful control of all the paper work related to purchasing. The main requirement is a kind of custodial care to see that nothing goes wrong. A long stay in these jobs is enough to break the spirit of a promising top-manager-to-be and train out his useful qualities. Toward the top we need a flexible man who will see the facts broadly, look into the future, and take risks boldly and well. These are not qualities bred in custodial jobs. Those jobs need to be filled and filled well, but not necessarily by the men we're training for top jobs. In the terminal middle-management jobs, we want men who are completely engrossed within the company—the sun rises and sets in the forms and practices of the XYZ Company. Toward the top we want men who can see beyond the company, who can see it in its broad social context, and who can imagine it doing something quite different and doing it quite differently. They are not necessarily the same men. Serving time in these jobs may have a rough social justice to "earn" promotion, but it is not necessarily good organizational practice. The fact that a man "came up the hard way" doesn't necessarily recommend this as a training ground for managers.

Job descriptions

One of the strongest weapons in maintaining centralized organizational control is the tight job description. When the organization was conceived, the whole job was broken up into rational parts which were put into little boxes as job descriptions on the chart. The job descriptions were made as full and explicit as possible and boundaries drawn around them to minimize the overlap from one man's job to the next. This served two purposes. First, it provided a neat centralized knowledge of where performance is expected, when that performance deviates from set standards, and the power to correct it. Second, the careful separation of jobs reduced the conflict in the organization. Clear-cut definition of the job minimizes conflicting interests. A strict hierarchical system minimizes conflict between levels. These steps tend to take the conflict out of the organization and put it into the individual. He resists the restriction of independence, initiative, and growth that goes with them. The result may be a loss, to the individual in terms of the conflict within himself, and to the organization in terms of the loss of breadth and initiative in the job.

The group model of organization suggests participation across levels, wide sharing of information, and the ability to influence upward as well as down in the hierarchy. The specification of jobs can be relaxed considerably. It can be done partly in general terms for a whole group and partly by the group itself. To achieve the broader sense of responsibility and commitment to general organizational goals, we need several people seeing the same thing that needs to be done. This puts some competition and initiative back into the system. It also puts some conflict back into it. But the organization's task must be partly to manage conflict and utilize it, not just to eliminate it. This does not mean giving up the hierarchical structure entirely or having an amorphous group of people who come to work and say "What'll we all do today?" But it may well be that a more fruitful position can be taken between the anarchy of the unorganized group and the rigid neatness of complete functional specialization. People are built in such a way that considerable return may flow from backing off a little from the tightest possible structure.

Managerial measurements and organization structure

It has been suggested that a modern view of an organization would be built on the integration of the group, their commitment, shared objectives, and mutual confidence and trust. If these are, in fact, major variables in the structure, we need better information about them. If each superior's first responsibilities are concerned with group building and the attitudes of his members, he needs measures of these things to tell him how he's doing. He needs these measures as a managerial tool to guide and evaluate his management practices on a day-to-day basis. If the commitment, self-control, and initiative of all the members of the organization are valuable assets of the company, their amount should be counted and accounted for; company policies should be examined and evaluated in terms of the way they increase, maintain, or dissipate this resource. Fortunately, the technology of the social sciences is such that it is completely possible to maintain a kind of constant inventory of these variables as a guide to management. In general, we haven't used them adequately. Management has, customarily, been content to measure the things that are easy to measure. These are usually cost, profit, and production. They are useful figures for a variety of purposes, but they are not necessarily the ideal indicators for guiding management practice. They are end-result variables that occur as a result of a number of other things. They are important to the business, but, to manage them effectively, we may also need measures of the things that lie behind them. To a much larger extent than we often realize, the choice of managerial strategies may be dictated by the kind of measurements we have chosen to make. Since this influence is often silent and hidden, we need to look at it in a little detail.

Job descriptions don't define jobs. Measurements do. Whatever the job description says, what a man does and what things he thinks are important on the job depend on the particular measurements that are taken of the job and the way they are used to evaluate performance. Aspects of the job which are not important enough for regular measurement tend to be ignored. If costs and production are regularly measured, they become the focal points. If group building is not measured, it tends to be ignored in favor of things that will show up in the measures—perhaps at the expense of the unmeasured variable. Most companies say that one aspect of every superior's job is to develop new managers from among his subordinates. Most companies don't measure the extent to which or the way in which this is successful. Most managers don't pay any attention to this responsibility. The measurements obtained define the job. If the measurements are inadequate, the concepts of the job and how to do it will be faulty and inadequate.

In broader terms, the information available to a company from its measurements shapes its management theory, and its management theory partly determines what measurements it will obtain. This circularity between strategy and information often locks management inside a narrow conception of objectives and accomplishments. Just as, in another context, it was suggested that organizations tend to create men in their own image, measurements tend to create organizations in *their* image. The measurements obtained reflect the management philosophy. They are interpreted in terms of this philosophy. They tend to validate the philosophy. There is little indication that other measurements would show a deficiency in the present strategy or would suggest the value of another approach to management.

To move ahead in organization theory, we need first to see the possibility of another view of the problem and then obtain the measures which will be relevant to an evaluation of it. If we are going to consider a theory of organization that rests on the structure of groups and the attitudes and behavior of their members, we need measures which will reflect these variables. Such measures will provide a tool to managers to evaluate and guide practice and decision making, and let them see the results of their leadership. They will let the company see the effect of alternative general approaches on attitudes and behavior and make it possible to see the relation between these variables and the end-result variables of costs and production. The measures are technically possible. Why don't we use them? In a strange way, personnel policies and general managerial philosophy have shown a degree of conservatism that would have been ruinous in the financial management of the business. We recognize risk taking as one of the essentials of the business operation with respect to capital improvements, product design, prices, and the like. But we have very little risk taking in the philosophy of management. Risk taking in business does not mean the blind following of a hunch and hoping it works. It is appropriate when accumulated evidence suggests a course of action has a good chance of proving fruitful, and when it can be tried out in such a way that careful check can be kept on the way it's working out. Both of these conditions seem to be met in the behavioral theory of the organization. It is clear that the pressures of society on the organization are changing and that new approaches are called for. Theory and research suggest possibilities in an approach to the organization through the social sciences and the study of behavior. At the same time, social science technology provides the techniques of measurement necessary to support and evaluate these approaches in practice. It is time to explore their possibility in action in the operation of the company.

The growth of organizations

Growth is a problem in most companies. With it comes the question, What happens to the organization as the company grows? Can it simply grow proportionately, or are there special organizational problems in organizational growth? If the organization grows all over at the same rate, it means that the shape of the structure remains the same. Changes in shape are a function of the relative size of the parts. If a company doubles in size by having two men in every place where one man stood before, it grows without changing shape. If some of the parts grow faster than others, the shape changes. The question is, Which type of growth is appropriate, and, if the latter, which parts grow faster?

Very few things can become larger effectively and stay the same shape. In general, with physical objects, as a thing gets bigger, if it stays the same shape it grows weaker. A bridge of a perfect shape won't work if it is made much bigger and kept the same shape. More and more of its strength goes into the job of holding itself up and less and less is available for its function as a bridge. A plank 10 feet long, 1 foot wide, and 1 inch thick will just about lie flat supported at both ends. One 100 feet long, 10 feet wide, and 10 inches thick would bend or break in the middle. To support its increased size, some of its dimensions must grow faster than others—its shape has to change. The same thing is probably true of companies.

The British biologist D'Arcy Thompson gives a nice example in living organisms in the story of Jack the Giant Killer. In the illustrations the giant is shown as looking like a man but ten times as big. Thompson points out that, in this case, Jack had nothing to fear. If the giant were ten times the size of a man, his weight would be a thousand times as great, since he increased in all dimensions. But a cross section of his bones, increasing in only two dimensions, would only be a hundred times as big. Consequently he would put ten times as much load on his bones at his size as a normal man would. Since human bones, in general, won't support ten times as much weight as they normally do, if the giant stood up, his legs would break. Jack was perfectly safe, protected by the fact that an increase in size without a change in shape is insupportable. The same thing is probably true of companies. How does it work out?

One more phenomenon from physical growth helps us to know what to look for in changes in shape as companies grow. In general, when objects change shape with increased size they become stronger at the point where the force tending to destroy the object is strongest. A shelf built out from the wall has a shelf bracket that is thickest right at the wall and tapers off further out; if a shelf breaks, the likeliest joint is right at the wall. The graceful bowstring arch on small bridges is not built that way for purely aesthetic reasons. It is strongest where the force tending to destroy the bridge is strongest. In general, the shape of the support for physical objects that have grown is a perfect diagram of the forces tending to destroy it. Similarly in a company. As the size changes, the shape must change. Some parts must grow faster than others. Those parts must grow fastest which resist the forces tending to destroy the organizations which are threatened by increasing size. We have already spoken of the tendency for organizations to fly apart because they are made of collections of individuals. To combat this with increased size we generally see a rapid growth of functions associated with organization building and communication. Also, needs for specialized skills develop as a result of size— labor relations, accounting, marketing, and the like—and these grow faster. In the early stages of growth the staff functions grow faster than the line and become a larger and larger proportion of the whole until their percentage of the total usually levels off and remains relatively constant for the rest of the life of the company. These things are not exactly the same from company to company, but a measure of this sort and the view of the problem that lies behind it can help us see, in a particular organization, where the forces threatening the organization are greatest.

As an organization grows it almost inevitably faces the

problem of decentralization. Today in most large firms it is fashionable to praise the virtues of decentralization. The word, however, doesn't always have the same meaning. For this reason, what seems like failure to one man may be success to another. The difference usually becomes apparent at an early stage in the process. When decentralization begins, we soon face the question, "Does decentralization include the autonomy, at lower levels, to run a centralized show?" It certainly often happens that an executive pushes authority and responsibility down to a subordinate who gathers more and more of them to himself to operate a tighter and tighter organization below himself. This isn't necessarily wrong, but it may disturb the superior who initiated the process, depending on what his original goal was. He now wonders, Can he pull back the autonomy and order the subordinate to push decentralization down further? Or will this centralized intervention to further decentralization destroy the decentralization?

Some firms aim at decentralization fairly simply as a response to size. The front office chooses to act as a kind of financial holding company, giving subordinate managers virtually complete autonomy and holding them responsible for little more than a profitable operation of their sector. Other firms want decentralization to provide initiative through a greater sense of participation, commitment, an acceptance of system-wide responsibility, and a feeling of shared objectives. Between these two there is a wide difference. In the second case, the tendency for autonomy to stop at the level immediately below the decision to decentralize is indeed a failure. The two types of decentralization must be approached differently. Decentralization in response to size can be accomplished by centralized order— "Effective at 0800 tomorrow we will be decentralized." The other kind requires a long and careful process. Executives must be retrained or created to handle it. Systems of reward must be rethought or overhauled. Traditional controls (budget and production) must be relinquished and information provided at lower levels. The new philosophy of management must be widely, slowly, and carefully shared throughout the organization. The two processes are so different that it is a pity they share the same name. Certainly the goals and processes of one will be a shock to an executive who thought in terms of the other.

A final problem that the question of decentralization brings up is the cost of the organization itself. If we shift a little from the decentralization of authority to the decentralization of decision making, the organizational cost becomes clear. Most decentralized firms retain a good deal of the business decision in the central office. For example, geographically dispersed managers may be restricted in independent authority for purchasing, accepting orders, setting prices, and the like. Otherwise two managers, acting in ignorance of each other, might compete with one another, overload the firm's production capacity, overcommit cash, or fail to take advantage of geographical differences in the market among either producers or consumers. For these reasons, to take advantage of the center's overview of both situations, the final decision tends to be retained at the home office. Under some circumstances, however, these factors —the probability of price variations, the profitability of contracting to purchase or produce—are stable enough so that decision rules can be set up telling the centralized subordinates how to operate in certain circumstances. To the extent that this is possible, it focuses attention on the alternative— maintaining a centralized decision-making operation. Now we have to ask, "What is the organization cost of the centralized style?" The cost of the organization may be more than the advantage gained from the single overview. For example, in a large retail operation, branch managers have relatively local price problems, what one manager does has little influence on another's action, and the probability of straining the company in money or production is low. In this situation a great deal of decentralization of decision making is possible, as in the classic Sears Roebuck case. Other cases may have much more interdependence of managers' actions, highly correlated prices across areas, and a tight supply of centralized production. In this case centralized structures would be worth a good deal. But we should begin to count the organizational cost to choose realistically between the cases where it is worth much or little. In general, this organization cost is one that we haven't measured. In addition to specifying clearly the objectives of the organization and measuring its effectiveness, it is time to begin to assess its cost.

SUMMARY

1. The world is changing. With it go changes in the pressures that are put on business for organization. To survive as a social institution, business must be responsive and adaptive to the changing pressures.

2. We need to answer more clearly the questions: What are the objectives of an organization? How do you tell a good organization plan when you see one? What is organized in an organization?

3. The traditional organization theory is based on a model which grew out of accounting and industrial engineering. Developments in research and theory in the social sciences make it possible to frame an alternative based on the model of the human group.

4. In a group-based model we move toward a point where the source of authority is in the group itself. The ultimate control is self-control. This depends on commitment, which in turn depends on integration. Under these circumstances

there is reason to believe that the total amount of influence or authority in the system can be expanded.

5. We have traditionally measured the things that are easy to measure. These are primarily budget and production data. A firm's philosophy and a manager's practices flow from measurements. Measurements define jobs more than job descriptions do. Social science technology now makes available measures related to attitudes, group strength, initiative, and commitment. To build an adaptive organization these data are essential.

6. As an organization grows its shape has to change. The parts that grow fastest should be those that maximally resist forces tending to destroy the organization as it grows.

7. Decentralization raises the question of organization cost. At what expense do we maintain centralized organization? At what return? Finally, to understand a particular decentralization the goals of different types must be understood.

INDEX

231